Real Exchange Rate Movements

Contributions to Economics

Gerhard Gehrig/Wladyslaw Welfe (Eds.)
Economies in Transition
1993. ISBN 3-7908-0721-4

Christoph M. Schneider
Research and Development Management: From the Soviet Union to Russia
1994. ISBN 3-7908-0757-5

Bernhard Böhm/Lionello F. Punzo (Eds.)
Economic Performance
1994. ISBN 3-7908-0811-3

Lars Olof Persson/Ulf Wiberg
Microregional Fragmentation
1995. ISBN 3-7908-0855-5

Ernesto Felli/Furio C. Rosati/Giovanni Tria (Eds.)
The Service Sector: Productivity and Growth
1995. ISBN 3-7908-0875-X

Giuseppe Munda
Multicriteria Evaluation in Fuzzy Environment
1995. ISBN 3-7908-0892-X

Boris Maurer
R & D, Innovation and Industrial Structure
1996. ISBN 3-7908-0900-4

Giovanni Galizzi/Luciano Venturini (Eds.)
Economics of Innovation: The Case of Food Industry
1996. ISBN 3-7908-0911-X

David T. Johnson
Poverty, Inequality and Social Welfare in Australia
1996. ISBN 3-7908-0942-X

Rongxing Guo
Border-Regional Economics
1996. ISBN 3-7908-0943-8

Oliver Fratzscher
The Political Economy of Trade Integration
1996. ISBN 3-7908-0945-4

Ulrich Landwehr
Industrial Mobility and Public Policy
1996. ISBN 3-7908-0949-7

Arnold Picot/Ekkehard Schlicht (Eds.)
Firms, Markets, and Contracts
1996. Corr. 2nd printing 1997.
ISBN 3-7908-0947-0

Karin Peschel (Ed.)
Regional Growth and Regional Policy Within the Framework of European Integration
1997. ISBN 3-7908-0957-8

Thorsten Wichmann
Agricultural Technical Progress and the Development of a Dual Economy
1997. ISBN 3-7908-0960-8

Ulrich Woitek
Business Cycles
1997. ISBN 3-7908-0997-7

Michael Carlberg
International Economic Growth
1997. ISBN 3-7908-0995-0

Massimo Filippini
Elements of the Swiss Market for Electricity
1997. ISBN 3-7908-0996-9

Giuseppe Gaburro (Ed.)
Ethics and Economics
1997. ISBN 3-7908-0986-1

Frank Hoster/Heinz Welsch/Christoph Böhringer
CO_2 Abatement and Economic Structural Change in the European Internal Market
1997. ISBN 3-7908-1020-7

Christian M. Hafner
Nonlinear Time Series Analysis with Applications to Foreign Exchange Rate Volatility
1997. ISBN 3-7908-1041-X

Sardar M.N. Islam
Mathematical Economics of Multi-Level Optimisation
1998. ISBN 3-7908-1050-9

Sven-Morten Mentzel

Real Exchange Rate Movements

An Econometric Investigation into Causes of Fluctuations in Some Dollar Real Exchange Rates

With 13 Figures
and 43 Tables

Physica-Verlag
A Springer-Verlag Company

Series Editors
Werner A. Müller
Martina Bihn

Author
Dr. Sven-Morten Mentzel
Martin-Luther-Str. 7
D-79312 Emmendingen, Germany

ISBN 3-7908-1081-9 Physica-Verlag Heidelberg New York

Cataloging-in-Publication Data applied for
Die Deutsche Bibliothek – CIP-Einheitsaufnahme
Mentzel, Sven-Morten: Real exchange rate movements: an econometric investigation into causes of fluctuations in some dollar real exchange rates / Sven-Morten Mentzel. – Heidelberg: Physica-Verl., 1998
(Contributions to economics)
ISBN 3-7908-1081-9

Softcover Design: Erich Kirchner, Heidelberg

SPIN 10661078 88/2202-5 4 3 2 1 0 – Printed on acid-free paper

Preface

In the period of flexible nominal exchange rates since 1973 the mark/dollar, pound/dollar, and yen/dollar real exchange rate have been fluctuating very much. Many economists assume that the fluctuations in these real exchange rates have had adverse effects on employment, inflation, allocation and growth in the corresponding countries and that they initiated protectionist measures. Therefore, it is interesting to investigate the causes of the fluctuations in the above mentioned dollar real exchange rates in order to determine appropriate policy recommendations to reduce these movements. One aim of this dissertation is therefore to examine the causes of fluctuations in the mark/dollar, pound/dollar, and yen/dollar real exchange rates for the period 1972-1994 with quarterly data. To reach this aim a two-country overshooting model for real exchange rates with government expenditure was estimated with Johansen's maximum likelihood cointegration procedure. The time series properties of the variables of each overshooting model for the three real exchange rates, which were ascertained by the unit root test of Elliott, Rothenberg, and Stock, made the application of Johansen's maximum likelihood cointegration procedure necessary. After having determined the number of cointegrating vectors with Johansen's cointegration tests, some of Johansen's tests were applied to the parameters of the three error correction models. These tests allow discovering which of the fundamentals had at least some effects on the three considered real exchange rates in the short-run or medium term. In order to figure out which of the fundamentals also had a long-run influence on the three real exchange rates, a factor model by Gonzalo and Granger was estimated. The factor analysis is based on the cointegration analysis. The factor model decomposes the variables of the overshooting model into a permanent and transitory (covariance-stationary) component in a multivariate framework. As will be seen, the permanent component of a real exchange rate can be interpreted as a fundamental real exchange rate in Gonzalo and Granger's factor model. A likelihood ratio test, constructed by Gonzalo and Granger, makes it possible to test, which of the fundamentals had also a long-run influence on the considered real exchange rates. The results of these tests have some importance insofar as a system of limited nominal exchange rate movements is problematic if real variables such as real government expenditure had some long-run influence on the three real exchange rates. Because of the interpretation of the permanent components the transitory components of the three real exchange rates consist of real exchange movements caused by innovations ("news") with respect to fundamentals on the one hand. On the other hand, they can consist of stationary "excessive" real exchange movements. In this paper "excessive" real exchange rate movements are defined as real exchange rate movements that are beyond the forward looking solution of the two-country overshooting model. That part of the transitory components of the three real exchange rates that is due to "news" was determined. The "rest" of the real exchange movements in one transitory component was interpreted as excessive. From the causes of the fluctuations in the three real exchange rates, monetary policy conclusions were drawn for reform of the three exchange rate systems. Furthermore, the forecast precision of the overshooting model in error correction form was compared with that of the simple random walk.

A further aim of this work is to investigate whether the three real exchange rates are covariance-stationary or not and to which extent they are covariance-stationary. The unit root test by Elliott, Rothenberg and Stock and a test for trivial cointegrating vectors, constructed by Johansen, will allow testing for non-stationarity and covariance-stationarity, respectively, of the three real exchange rates. The factor model by Gonzalo and Granger makes it possible to find out to which extent the three real exchange rates are covariance-stationary.

I would like to thank Professor Siegfried Hauser (supervisor) and Professor Dietrich Lüdeke for their guidance and valuable comments. For financial aid and academic advice I am very much indebted to my esteemed Professor Hans-Hermann Francke. I am also grateful for helpful suggestions by Professor Oliver Landmann (Albert-Ludwigs-University at Freiburg), Professor Jesus Gonzalo (Boston University), Professor Søren Johansen (Institute of Mathematical Statistics in Kopenhagen), Professor Manfred Willms (Christian-Albrechts-University at Kiel), and Professor Werner Gaab (Universität Gesamthochschule Essen). Moreover, I received useful comments from my colleagues Bernhard Pfaff and Dr. Michael Pflüger.

My mother Rita Schächtle provided much financial support and encouragement during my dissertation. In particular, she paid a very expensive stay of the author at the Department of Economics at the University of Pennsylvania at Philadelphia. Without the studies at the University of Pennsylvania, the author would not have been able to write this dissertation.

Finally, I want to thank all my friends in Germany (Martin Dilger, Stefan Beste, Lothar Scherer, Gerhard Lickert, Martin Ohmer, and Andrea and Bill Buhler) and in the US (Michael Binder, Jose Lopez, Nachiket Mor, Per

Fredriksson, and Kamal Saggi) for much encouragement in the last 5 years. They were always able to cheer me up during difficult phases of my dissertation. Special thanks go to Andrea and Bill Buhler and Martin Dilger who read the manuscript for typographical errors. Of course, any remaining errors are mine.

Table of Contents

Page

A. Motivation

One aim of this work is to investigate the causes of fluctuations in the mark/dollar, pound/dollar, and yen/dollar real exchange rates. These real exchange rates have had been fluctuating to a large extent since the beginning of the period of flexible exchange rates in 1973 (see figure 1). Generally, it is assumed that these movements had bad effects on employment, inflation, allocation and growth in the industrialized countries and that they initiated protectionist measures[1]. Therefore several proposals have been made to reduce these fluctuations.

A second aim of this paper is to choose one among these proposals on the basis of the analysis of the causes of the fluctuations in the three real exchange rates. The various proposals differ from each other in two aspects: The first aspect concerns the question of whether governments and central banks are willing to use macroeconomic policies to reduce real exchange rate movements. The second aspect is related to the causes of real exchange rate movements.

One group in the debate about the reform of exchange rate systems for the three real exchange rates assumes that current or unanticipated changes in fundamentals in the future, especially changes in monetary and fiscal variables, are responsible for the fluctuations in the above mentioned three real exchange rates. This group can be divided into two subgroups according to the first aspect mentioned above. The first subgroup tries to reduce real exchange movements by making monetary and fiscal policies more stable[2] or by improving the coordination of fiscal and monetary policies among countries[3]. Friedman (1953) can also be included in this subgroup since he also believed

[1]Marston 1988, p. 89–96, and Williamson, 1985, p. 38–46 give an overview over these effects.

[2]The expression "more stable" has two meanings: On the one hand, it means that monetary and fiscal policies should not get "excessive" in one or the other direction. On the other hand, it means that they should be more or less foreseeable.

[3]Members of this group are, for example, Branson (1985), Dornbusch/Frankel, 1987, p. 50, Feldstein (1986), Frenkel/Mussa, 1980, p. 379–380, Frenkel, 1985, p. 17–18, 1987, p. 207–208, Landmann (1988), Obstfeld, 1985, p. 443. Landmann (1988) used a model with a medium-term framework. According to Dornbusch and Frankel, 1987, p. 25, fundamentals and exchange rates are only related to each other in the long-run.

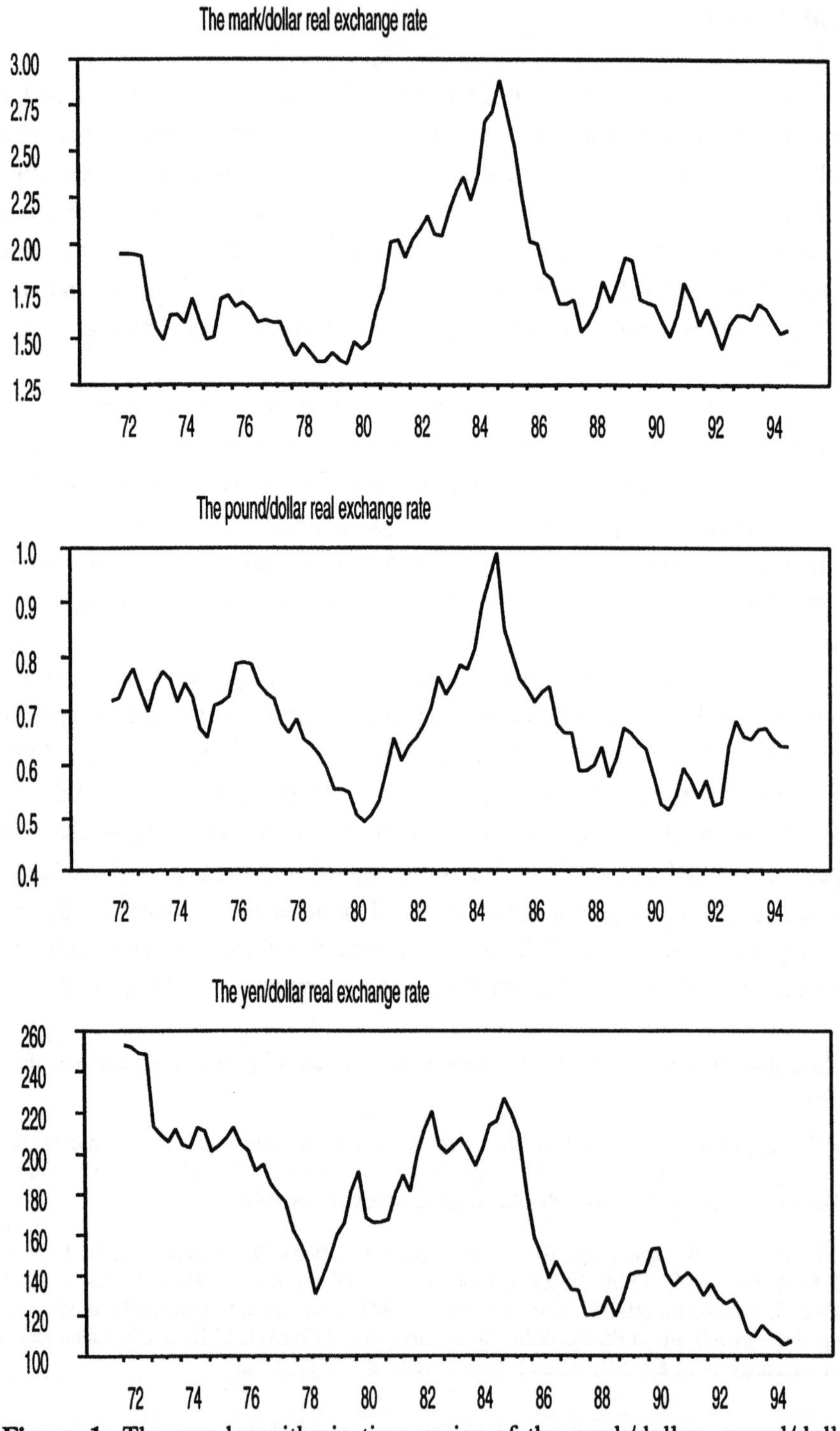

Figure 1: The non logarithmic time series of the mark/dollar, pound/dollar, and yen/dollar real exchange rate

in fundamentals as main determinants of exchange rates. He wrote[4]: "A flexible exchange rate need not to be an unstable exchange rate. If it is, it is primarily because there is underlying instability in the economic conditions governing international trade." According to Friedman, the economic conditions which govern international trade are, for example, weather, technical conditions of production, consumer tastes, and the like[5]. Other conditions which govern international trade are monetary conditions, such as divergent degrees of inflation or deflation in various countries[6]. Friedman also argued that there might be speculative deviations from the fundamental rates[7]. But speculation will be stabilizing. After a short time the exchange rate will return to its fundamental rate. Speculators, who behave destabilizingly, will disappear from the market over time.

The second subgroup in the first main group assumes that governments and members of central banks are not willing to implement more stable fiscal and monetary policies voluntarily in order to reduce real exchange rate movements. They would always have an incentive to change real exchange rates through changes in macro policies to reach positive employment effects in their countries. According to this subgroup governments and central banks also have often their own economics policy conceptions. Thus they are often unwilling to use monetary and fiscal policies to reduce real exchange rate movements when the required measures are not compatible with their economics policy aims. Therefore, the second subgroup[8] demands the implementation of a system of limited exchange rate flexibility so that governments and central banks are forced to carry out macroeconomic policies which are consistent with real exchange stability. However, systems with limited exchange rate flexibility are problematic when there are real shocks (government expenditure shocks or real income shocks) with permanent effects on real exchange rates[9]. Several allocative reasons can be given for this argument. The

---

[4]See Friedman, 1953, p. 173. Johnson, 1972, p. 208, 213, took the same view as Friedman.

[5]See Friedman, 1953, p. 159.

[6]See Friedman, 1953, p. 159.

[7]See Friedman, 1953, p. 159.

[8]See, for the example, the proposal of McKinnon (1988) and the target zone proposal of Miller and Williamson (1987).

[9]Obstfeld, 1985, p. 387–410, made this point in a two-country Keynesian model with

first reason can be made clear within the framework of Dornbusch's overshooting model for a small country with perfect foresight with respect to the price level, and government expenditure but with fixed exchange rates. In this model the expected exchange rate changes are zero and the overshooting model reduces to an autonomous first-order difference equation[10]. In the "overshooting" model with fixed exchange rates model, an increase in government expenditure leads to slowly rising prices and therefore to real appreciations of the home currency over time because this model assumes a full employment economy. The rising prices reduce real money supply and cause the nominal interest rate to go up. The rising nominal interest rate entails capital imports and a nominal appreciation of the home currency. Since the central bank of the home country has to buy foreign currency to keep the nominal rate fixed, money supply increases. The rising money supply reduces nominal interest rates until they reach again their initial level which is equal to the nominal foreign interest rate. It can be easily shown that the long-run real exchange rate is the same as in Dornbusch's model with flexible nominal exchange rates. Thus the real exchange rate is neither constant in the short-run nor in the long-run in a fixed exchange rate system. The real appreciation is necessary to get aggregate demand equal to aggregate supply after the occurence the positive government expenditure shock. Since an increase of government expenditure just leads to a nominal appreciation without price changes in Dornbusch's model with flexible exchange rates, nominal exchange rate flexibility is completely replaced by price variability in Dornbusch's model with fixed exchange rates.

Negative permanent real income shocks with respect to full employment output also cause permanent real exchange rate changes through increases in domestic prices in Dornbusch's model with fixed nominal exchange rates in the long-run. The real appreciation of the home currency is again necessary to get aggregate demand equal to aggregate supply. The same holds in Dornbusch's model with flexible exchange rates in the long-run. In this model exogenous shocks with respect to full employment output also cause prices to increase in the long-run. But, in addition, as can be shown, there is some nominal appreciation in the long-run which leads to the needed real appreciation. This

---

variable output.

[10]For an overshooting model in discrete time with flexible exchange rates, see Azariadis, 1993, p. 46-51. This model can be reduced to a first-order difference equation by setting the expected exchange rate changes to zero.

nominal appreciation is necessary since increases in domestic prices lead to proportional nominal exchange rate changes in Dornbusch's model in the long-run[11]. That is, the real exchange rate does not change when domestic prices change. This implies that some nominal appreciation is still needed to get some real appreciation in the long-run and to equalize aggregate demand and supply.

In summary, in case of permanent real shocks a system of fixed exchange rates leads to a higher price variability than a system of nominal exchange rate flexibility. This argument can probably be taken over to systems of limited exchange rate flexibility (target zones, gold standard, fixed exchange rates systems with narrow bands) in general although the above argument is strictly only valid for absolutely fixed exchange rates. The problem with the higher price variability is that it involves welfare losses since deviations from target inflation rates increase. This problem diminishes the wider the exchange rate bands are.

Nominal exchange rate flexibility is also desired for another allocative reason when real exchange rates are determined by permanent changes of real variables. In this case, nominal exchange movements replace the lack of price flexibility in goods markets. If the nominal exchange rate were not flexible enough, the sluggish price movement would have adverse effects on allocation. Friedman (1953, p. 173) also showed with his well-known daylight saving time parable that nominal exchange rate variability is preferred to price variability for allocative reasons. According to Feldstein (1994, p. 69), nominal exchange rate flexibility is also needed for allocative reasons when budget deficits have permanent effects on real exchange rates in a full employment economy. He wrote[12]:

> "Moreover, even if the real value of the dollar could have been reduced, I worried that lowering the dollar without shrinking the

---

[11]The long-run nominal exchange rate is: $\bar{s} = \bar{p} - p^* + 1/\delta(\bar{y} + \sigma i^* - u)$. See for this equation Azariadis, 1993, p. 47. The variables have the following meanings: $\bar{s}$ = nominal long-run exchange rate, $\bar{p}$ = long-run domestic price level, p^* = the given foreign price level, $\bar{y}$ = domestic full employment output, i^* = foreign nominal interest rate, u = real government expenditure. The parameters δ and σ are positive in sign. The domestic price level leads to proportional changes in the nominal exchange rate. Thus the real exchange rate stays constant when there are price level changes. The term $1/\delta\,\bar{y}$ causes the necessary real appreciation. That is the nominal exchange rate takes over still some of the needed real adjustment even though it could rise in the long-run when the positive change in $\bar{p}$ is greater than the negative change in $1/\delta\,\bar{y}$ when negative permanent income shocks occur.

[12]See Feldstein, 1994, p. 69–70.

budget deficit would have been counterproductive. A lower dollar would have meant a smaller trade deficit, but that would have meant a smaller gap between saving and investment. With nothing done to increase saving, the level of domestic investment in the United States would have been declined. Lowering the dollar without shrinking the budget deficit would have reduced the pain felt by exporters and by those who competed with imports but only by transferring the pain to the other sectors of the economy that were directly sensitive to higher interest rates. If anything, without the trade deficit, the crowding out caused by the budget deficit would have been concentrated on a smaller number of industries and, therefore, even more painful. Moreover, the reduced level of investment in plant and equipment would have left the economy in a worse position in future years.

In short, the trade deficit was a safety valve by which the pressures caused by a massive budget deficit could be partly reduced through the resulting inflow of capital. The inflow of capital was the natural market response to the fall in national saving. There seemed to be no reason to believe that shrinking the trade deficit without lowering the budget deficit would represent an improved allocation of resources [footnote left out]".

A similar argument could be made for rising government expenditure. In a full employment economy, an increase in government expenditure would also lead to higher interest rates if the trade deficit were missing as a safety valve because a system of limited nominal exchange rate flexibility prevented a real appreciation of the home currency.

As Obstfeld (1985, p. 407) points out, some limitation of nominal exchange rate flexibility would be justified when real shocks only have transitory effects on real exchange rates. In this case, the real exchange rate would be kept more or less constant by monetary policy in the short-run until the effects of the real shock have died out.

It is easy to see in this simple model that a system of fixed exchange rate flexibility avoids a higher price variability when monetary shocks occur. The reason is that the domestic central bank always keeps the nominal home interest rate at the level of the given foreign nominal interest rate through intervention in the foreign exchange market. Hence, there are no interest rate and nominal exchange rate changes and no demand, price and real exchange rate changes can take place.

Proponents of systems with limited nominal exchange rate flexibility also recognized the need for adjustments of fixed or target rates when real shocks have permanent effects on real exchange rates[13]. Therefore, they advocate parity adjustments when these kinds of shock occur. But the experience with the Bretton-Woods system shows that governments were often not willing to devaluate their currencies when this was necessary. Recently, this experience was also made within the European Monetary System (EMS) in 1989[14]. In 1989, the German Bundesbank forecasted rising German government expenditure because of the German reunification. Thus the Bundesbank advocated a nominal appreciation of the mark in the European Monetary System. But parity changes had to be agreed unanimously. The British government was against a devaluation of the pound because it feared a credibility loss of its monetary strategy. France refused to devaluate the Franc for purely political reasons. Since government expenditure rose tremendously in Germany, the necessary adjustments of real exchange rates had to be brought about by deflations in the EMS member countries. Because the Bundesbank performed a strict anti-inflation policy in the nineties, the necessary real appreciation had to be caused by one-sided strong deflations in the other EMS countries. In addition, Krugman (1989b, p. 71) suspects that parity adjustments might lead to speculative attacks since speculators will try to anticipate devaluations. For example, it is argued that the above mentioned non-adjustment of parity rates in the EMS caused the speculative crisis within the EMS in September 1992[15].

In summary, a system of limited nominal exchange rate flexibility seems problematic if real shocks have permanent effects on real exchange rates and if parity adjustments are not made. Although real exchange rate movements can not be reduced in a system of flexible nominal exchange rates when permanent real shocks are present this system is the "lesser evil" than a system of limited exchange rate flexibility. Assume that fiscal policies of two countries

[13]See for example Krugman, 1989b, p. 71 or Williamson (1985, p. 16). Williamson pleads for adjustments of parity rates when there are real shocks such as differential productivity growth in different countries, exploitation of new resource discoveries, and permanent exogenous changes in the terms of trade.

[14]Eichengreen and Wypolsz, 1993, p. 77, made the following argument in another context.

[15]For a discussion of this claim see Eichengreen and Wyplosz, 1993, p. 73-82.

are the only real variables which influenced real exchange rates in the long-run. A system of limited nominal exchange rate flexibility should also be rejected in this case if fiscal policies are not disciplined in a system of limited exchange rate flexibility and if parity adjustments are not carried out when fiscal shocks arise.

The framework of the overshooting model might be criticized as being too simple. However, McKibbin and Sachs (1988) used a generalized multi-country overshooting model to evaluate the effects of different variants of flexible and fixed exchange rate systems on important target variables[16] by simulation. Although the framework of the overshooting model is very simple, a part of its basic policy conclusions seems to hold in more complicated overshooting models. McKibbin and Sachs (1988, p. 409) wrote:

> "Using a dynamic general equilibrium simulation model of the world economy, we have shown that the performance of each regime depends crucially on the nature of the shocks impinging on the economy. For the country-specific shocks considered above[17], the fixed exchange rate regimes perform poorly in the sense of leading to a large variance of a set of macroeconomic target variables. When a shock requires adjustment of the real exchange rate, a regime of fixed nominal exchange rates in a sticky price world leads to short-term non-adjustment of the real exchange rate which results in increased variance of target variables. .... For other shocks, such as negatively correlated monetary shocks, the fixed exchange rate system regime proposed by McKinnon performs well, especially if the shock is unobserved."

That is, a fixed exchange rate system does not necessarily lead to better results as the overshooting model suggested when there are monetary shocks. At least, one of the above policy conclusions of the overshooting model is still valid with respect to relatively persistent real demand shocks. It has to be qualified that McKibbin and Sachs have not considered target zones. They

[16]McKibbin and Sachs' target variables are inflation rates, income variables, current account-gross-domestic-product ratios, and budget deficit-ratios.

[17]McKibbin and Sachs (1988) considered relatively persistent demand shocks, temporary portfolio shifts from the US to Europe and Japan as well as temporary price level and money demand shocks, which all had permanent effects via the dynamics of the model.

have not investigated either the effect of country specific income shocks on target variables.

From the above arguments, it can be seen that it is important to know whether real variables had permanent effects on the mark/dollar, pound/dollar, and yen/dollar real exchange rate. The author will test within the framework of a factor model by Gonzalo and Granger whether this holds.

The second main group assumes that most of the fluctuations in the three real exchange rates are of excessive nature. Excessive real exchange rate fluctuations are defined in this paper as real exchange rate movements which are beyond the forward-looking solution of a structural exchange rate model for real exchange rates[18]. Members of this group plead for a transactions tax[19] on foreign exchange or for the introduction of a dual exchange rate system. Williamson (1985) and Miller and Williamson (1987) advocate the implementation of a target zone for the important real exchange rates such as the above mentioned real exchange rates. Thus the Miller-Williamson proposal can be put into the second subgroup of the first main group and into the second main group. Probably, it belongs more in the second main group since Miller and Williamson consider most of the fluctuations in the dollar real exchange rate as excessive. Krugman (1989a, p. 102, 104, 105, 1989b, p. 71) also recommends a target zone with published and adjustable nominal target rates in case of real shocks. In his opinion, some of the real exchange rate movements are also of excessive nature. Furthermore, nonsterilized and sterilized interventions in the foreign exchange market belong to the proposals in this group. According to the proponents of the second main group, the avoidance of "excessive" monetary and fiscal policies and the coordination of fiscal and monetary policies would be helpful in stabilizing real exchange rates but these measures are not sufficient to reduce real exchange movements to a greater extent.

Recently several theories have been developed to explain excessive exchange rate movements. Although most of the models for these theories refer to nominal exchange rate movements their conclusions also hold for real exchange rates since nominal and real exchange rates are highly correlated. The development of the theories for excessive exchange rate movements was motivated by the fact that the monetary models with sluggish prices and the

---

[18] See for this definition Williamson, 1985, p. 16–17, p. 51. Williamson, 1985, p. 13–15, also defines "excessivity" in other ways.

[19] See the proposal of Tobin (1978). Dornbusch, 1982, p. 595–596, suggested the introduction of an real interest equalization tax which equalizes real interest differentials between assets in different currencies.

"news" approach were not compatible with biased forecast errors for many dollar exchange rates[20] and that risk premia could not explain these biases[21]. In addition, monetary models even if they are extended with time varying exogenous fundamentals - the monetary models with "news" - could not explain some developments of the dollar exchange rate in the eighties. This is true for the real appreciation of the dollar between the middle of 1984 and February 1985 and for the dollar appreciation between 1988 and 1989. This also motivated the development of the theories of excessive foreign exchange movements. The models for excessive exchange rate rate movements can be divided into two groups. One group extends the "news" approach and assumes rational exchange rate expectations. Excessive exchange movements by rational speculative bubbles, Peso problems[22] and learning processes[23] belong to this group. Probably, exchange rate changes caused by announced changes of stochastic processes for exogenous fundamentals ("regime shifts") can also be included in this group[24]. The second group assumes that market participants have irrational exchange rate expectations. Dornbusch (1982, p. 587–589), Krugman (1985), and Frankel and Froot (1993b) constructed models with this kind of excessive exchange rate movements.

The third main group considers real exchange rate movements as a reaction to an optimal adjustment of households and firms to real shocks[25]. The theoretical basis of this group are intertemporal equilibrium models with flexible prices. The real exchange rate changes are desired if the shocks, which caused these movements, are desired from a welfare perspective. An intervention in the foreign exchange rate market would cause no changes in real

---

[20]Levich (1985, 1989) and Frankel and Froot (1987) showed that forecast errors were biased for many nominal dollar exchange rates. In addition, Frankel and Froot (1987) used survey data to demonstrate the biases in forecast errors for many nominal dollar exchange rates.

[21]See the empirical studies of Frankel (1982, 1985), Lewis (1988a), Hodrick/Srivastava (1984), and Frankel/Froot (1993a).

[22]Lewis (1992) shows how peso problems can emerge.

[23]Lewis (1988b, 1989ab) developed exchange rate models with learning processes.

[24]For an example, see Blanchard/Fischer, 1989, p. 219. Their example is related to Cagan's money demand function. This example can easily be extended to foreign exchange rates. Flood and Hodrick, 1986, p. 837–839, give another example in the framework of an intertemporal asset pricing model.

[25]See for example Stockman (1987, 1990).

exchange rates and would lead to allocative distortions. This group pleads for a system of flexible exchange rates. An empirical implication of these models is that real exchange rates should follow random walks. In this paper, unit root tests will be conducted to test for random walk behavior of the three considered real exchange rates.

The question arises which of the first three proposals should be accepted. To answer this question the author uses Johansen's maximum likelihood procedure to estimate a two-country overshooting model in error correction form with real government expenditure. The exchange rate models refer to the mark/dollar, pound/dollar, and yen/dollar real exchange rate. The cointegration analysis will then be the basis for the application of the factor model of Gonzalo and Granger (1995). This model decomposes all variables of one exchange rate model into permanent and transitory components. The factor model makes it possible to find out which fundamentals also had permanent effects on all three considered real exchange rates in the long-run. It was pointed out above that a system of limited nominal exchange rate flexibility would be problematic if real shocks had permanent effects on real exchange rates.

The permanent component of a real exchange rate can be interpreted as the fundamental rate in Gonzalo and Granger's factor model. Correspondingly, the transitory component of one real exchange rate can then in part or completely consist of covariance-stationary excessive real exchange movements on the one hand. The identification of the transitory component of one real exchange rate with excessive real exchange rate movements is for some kinds of excessive real exchange rate movements just a thinkable possibility since this paper will not test for existence or non existence of all sorts of excessive real exchange rate movements. On the other hand, the transitory component can consist of covariance-stationary real exchange movements caused by "news" and by expected changes in exogenous fundamentals according to their stochastic processes. In order to be able to choose between the proposals of the first two main groups it is necessary to know how much "news" and expected changes in exogenous fundamentals caused changes in the transitory components of the three real exchange rates. The reason is that these causes of real exchange rate movements are not seen as reasons for reforming exchange rate systems[26]. The basic policy recommendation of the "news" approach is that

[26]See for this view Frenkel/Mussa, 1980, p. 379–280.

monetary and fiscal policy should become more stable or less erratic[27]. The proportion of the transitory component of one real exchange rate which is due to expected changes of exogenous fundamentals was not estimated. It would have been difficult to determine this proportion within the factor model. In addition, the proportion of expected nominal exchange rate changes is small in comparison with the total monthly or quarterly change of nominal exchange rate according to Mussa (1979, p. 177). Mussa called the low proportion of expected nominal exchange rates an empirical regularity of nominal exchange rate movements. This empirical regularity is true for all exchange rates and all periods of flexible exchange rates. As was mentioned above, nominal and real exchange rates are highly correlated. This implies that this empirical regularity also holds for real exchange rates. Hence, only the proportion of real exchange movements in a transitory component of one real exchange rate that was due to "news" was estimated. Now the choice between the proposals of the first two main groups depends on the seize of the permanent component and the proportion of real exchange rate movements in the transitory components which are caused by "news". For example, if the permanent components and the proportion of real exchange movements in the transitory components caused by "news" were large, a reform of the three exchange rate movements would not be necessary. On the other hand, if the permanent components and the proportion of real exchange rate movements caused by "news" were small, the three exchange rate systems should be reformed.

It has been discussed in the empirical exchange theory literature whether real exchange rate theories are integrated (I(1)) or covariance-stationary (I(0)) processes or whether absolute or relative purchasing power parity holds in the long-run. Sometimes it is also claimed that some real exchange rates follow trend-stationary processes. Different methods have been applied to investigate these issues. Froot and Rogoff (1994) give an overview over the approaches to test for (trend-) stationarity of real exchange rates. This paper will use the factor model of Granger and Gonzalo (1995) to explore the covariance-stationarity or nonstationarity of real exchange rates. As was already mentioned this model decomposes the mark/dollar, pound/dollar, and yen/dollar real exchange rate into a permanent and transitory (covariance-stationary) component. The advantage of the factor model is that it also allows to determine the extent of covariance-stationarity of the three real exchange rates in a multivariate statistical model.

---

[27]See again, for example, Frenkel/Mussa, 1980, p. 379–380.

The rest of the paper is organized as follows. Section B. derives the real exchange rate equation which is estimated in error correction form in section D. It also describes the construction of the variables which are used for estimation. In section C., unit root tests are performed. The cointegration analysis is made in section D. Section E. uses the two-country overshooting model in error correction form for forecasting to evaluate the explanatory power of the overshooting model. The cointegration analysis in section D. is a prerequisite for the application of the factor model of Gonzalo and Granger (1995) in section F. Section G. draws conclusions.

B. The Two-Country Overshooting Model and Construction of Variables

In this paper, a two-country version of the Dornbusch (1976) open macroeconomics model with a free-floating exchange rate will be estimated. The model stems from Buiter (1988, p. 122) and is not reported here. Buiter did not derive an estimable equation for his two-country model. To get an estimable equation it was proceeded as follows: Buiter (1988, p. 124) derived the following equation for the long-run equilibrium real exchange rate:

$$(1) \qquad \bar{q}_t = \frac{1}{\Lambda}[\sigma u^* - \sigma^* u] + \frac{\sigma^* + \sigma\beta^*}{\Lambda}\bar{y} - \frac{\sigma + \sigma^*\beta}{\Lambda}\bar{y}^*.$$

q is the real exchange rate for the home currency (e.g. the real mark/dollar exchange rate). The variable u denotes again real government expenditure. $\bar{y}$ is real full employment output again. The variables with a star are foreign (US) variables. σ, β, Λ, and the corresponding parameters with a star are positive parameters. Meese and Rogoff (1988, p. 936) showed that the following equation holds for the Dornbusch model:

$$(2) \qquad q_t = \bar{q}_t + \psi(r_t - r_t^*).$$

r_t is the short-run real interest rate. ψ is a parameter which is smaller than -1. Substituting equation (1) into equation (2) gives:

$$(3) \qquad q_t = \frac{1}{\Lambda}(\sigma u^* - \sigma^* u) + \frac{\sigma^* + \sigma\beta^*}{\Lambda}\bar{y} - \frac{\sigma + \sigma^*\beta}{\Lambda}\bar{y}^* + \psi(r_t - r_t^*).$$

Since real interest parity might not hold[1], the following equation without symmetry restrictions was estimated in error correction form for the sample first quarter 1972 until fourth quarter 1994:

$$(4) \qquad q_t = \frac{1}{\Lambda}(\sigma u^* - \sigma^* u) + \frac{\sigma^* + \sigma\beta^*}{\Lambda}\bar{y} - \frac{\sigma + \sigma^*\beta}{\Lambda}\bar{y}^* + \psi' r_t - \psi^{*\prime} r_t^*.$$

---

[1]MacDonald and Taylor, 1992, p. 36–40, give an overview about different empirical investigations that could not validate uncovered and real interest parity.

The construction of the variables is as follows: The real exchange rates consist of nominal average exchange rates from the last month of one quarter and of the corresponding consumer price indices from both countries. The full employment output variables are approximated by real gross domestic (Germany, United Kingdom, USA) or real gross national product (Japan)[2]. Real government expenditure for each country is divided by real output. The government expenditure and output variables were divided by four when they were at annual rates. Short-term real interest rates are constructed from short-term nominal interest rates and the inflation rate of the current period. Thus it was assumed that market participants' inflationary expectations for the next period coincide with the current inflation rate. The annual short-run nominal interest rates were divided by four to get quarterly nominal interest rates. Like the real exchange rate nominal interest and inflation rates also refer to the last month of a quarter. All variables except interest rates are in logarithmic form. Appendix 2 describes the original time series.

---

[2]Gross domestic product will be abbreviated in the following with GDP, gross national product with GNP.

C. Tests for an Autoregressive Unit Root in the Variables of the Overshooting Model

In this section, a test of an autoregressive unit root by Elliott, Rothenberg, and Stock (1992) will be performed with respect to the variables in equation (4) from section B. The tests of an autoregressive unit root are necessary in order to decide whether a cointegration analysis is useful. If all variables were I(0) processes, the effort to specify an error correction model would not be necessary and "classical" methods could be applied. The tests of unit roots will also show which of the real exchange rates are I(1) or I(0) processes. The time series properties of real exchange rates are important to know for foreign exchange rate modelling. To model real exchange rates correctly their stochastic properties should be known. The results of these tests will also decide which error correction model should be used. For example, if several variables turn out to be trend-stationary, an error correction model (ECM) should be applied which allows for this kind of variables or more precisely which allows for stochastic cointegration[1].

The test from Elliott, Rothenberg, and Stock (=ERS) is a modification of the well-known Dickey-Fuller or more precisely the Dickey-Said test[2]. It detrends the variables with a variant of the GLS method. The Dickey-Fuller test just requires OLS-detrending. Because of these modifications they call their test Dickey-Fuller-GLS test. Stock (1992) has shown that this test has better power properties in finite samples than the Dickey-Said test and other unit root tests. The reason for the better power properties in finite samples comes from the fact that the power of the test reaches a so called asymptotic power envelope. Many unit root tests have less asymptotic power than the test from ERS. Moreover, the test takes over the good size properties of the Dickey-Fuller test.

The testing strategy of Perron (1988, p. 314–317) was applied while testing for unit roots. To avoid power losses this strategy suggests starting with the model with time trend. If the null hypothesis of a unit root for this model is rejected, no further steps are necessary. If the null hypothesis of a unit root is accepted for this model, the model with constant should be used for testing. If the null hypothesis of a unit root model for this model is

---

[1]Ogaki and Park (1990) coined this term.

[2]The Dickey-Said test was designed to test for an autoregressive unit root in ARMA processes. The Dickey-Fuller test just refers to autoregressive processes.

rejected, testing for a unit root can be stopped. For intuitive reasoning of this strategy see Perron (1988, p. 314–317). The model without constant was not used for most of the variables except for short-run real interest rates. This was done since the time series for most of the variables seemed to be better represented by a model with a time trend or with a constant. The number of lagged differences were chosen according to the recommendations of ERS. They recommended choosing the Bayesian information criterion (BIC). This criterion was used for the model with time trend and for the model with constant. The maximum number of lags was chosen to be 10. For the model without trend and without constant, the test of ERS reduces to the Dickey-Said test. To determine the number of lagged differences for this test Ng and Perron (1993) suggested using a sequential testing procedure. According to this procedure, a maximum number of lagged differences $k_{1,max}$ has to be determined first. Then a t-test has to applied to the parameter of the last lagged difference. If this parameter is significantly different from zero, the maximum number of lagged differences has to be accepted. If it is not different from zero, the parameter of the $k_{1,max}$ - 1 lagged difference has to be checked for significance, etc. Ng and Perron (1993) showed theoretically that the Dickey-Said "t"-statistic does have the asymptotic distribution of Dickey and Fuller (1979) when this testing procedure is used. They also showed with a simulation study that the sequential testing procedure leads to better finite sample properties in comparison with other selection criteria under which the "t"-statistic does also have the asymptotic distribution derived by Dickey and Fuller (1979).

The ERS-test has been applied by Cheung and Lai (1994) to several real exchange rates with consumer and wholesale price indices for the period 1900 to 1992. They used annual data and the model with time trend. They could reject the null hypothesis of a unit root for the three considered real exchange rates in this paper and for some other real exchange rates. One exception was the real mark/dollar rate when wholesale price indices were used. This paper will apply the ERS-test to the period first quarter 1972 to fourth quarter 1994. Tables 1 to 4 present the results of the unit root tests for the variables of the four countries. The letters a, b, c, d have the following meaning: a= significant at $\alpha = 10\%$, b = significant at $\alpha = 5\%$, c = significant at $\alpha = 2.5\%$, d = significant at $\alpha = 1\%$. The first number behind the values of the test statistics is the chosen number of lagged differences in the regressions. The second number is the effective number of observations taking into account the lost number of observations through lagged differences. Since the "t"-statistics of the ERS-Test for the model with and without constant have the asymptotic distributions for the model without constant and without trend, which were derived by Dickey and Fuller, the corresponding critical values in MacKinnon (1991) can be used for testing. The formulas of these critical values for the model without constant and trend are as follows: α = 1%: -2.5658 - 1.960/T -10.04/T^2; α = 5%: -1.9393 - 0.398/T; α = 10%: -1.6156 - 0.181/T. For the model with time trend the asymptotic distribution of the ERS-"t"-statistic differs from that of Dickey and Fuller. ERS have simulated the asymptotic distribution of the "t"-statistic for this model and computed the following critical values for a sample size of T = 100 (see ERS, 1992, p. 20): α = 10%: -2.74; α = 5%: -3.03; α = 2.5%: -3.29; α = 1%: -3.58.

I(1) processes are the yen/dollar real exchange rate (see table 3), the government expenditure-output ratios (see tables 1 to 4), the Japanese real GNP (see table 3) as well as the US short-run real interest rate (see table 4). The German real GDP has an explosive unit root when the model with constant was used for testing. Since explosive unit roots are usually not considered in economics, the model with constant is probably inappropriate for German real GDP. The results of the ERS-test for the model with constant and time trend indicate that the German real GDP is an I(1) variable with a time trend. Stationary around zero, around a constant or trend-stationary are the mark/dollar exchange rate, the pound/dollar real exchange rate, the German, British, and Japanese short-run real interest rates as well as the British and US GDP.

Since the graphs of the first differences of all variables looked stationary they seemed not to possess a second autoregressive unit root. Hence, a test for a second autoregressive unit root was not applied. Pantula (1989), for example, constructed such a test.

According to the test results for the mark/dollar and pound/dollar real exchange rate, relative purchasing power parity holds for these real exchange rates since these real exchange rates are stationary around a constant. It is not clear whether relative purchasing power parity holds for the yen/dollar real exchange rate since the null hypothesis of a unit root could not be rejected for the model with constant. The reason for this ambiguity is that changes in the yen/dollar real equilibrium exchange rate might have interrupted the relationship between price levels and the yen/dollar nominal exchange rate, that is, relative purchasing power parity might still hold because it is related to monetary factors.

	q_t	$u_t/\bar{y}_t$	$\bar{y}_t$	r_t
t_{ρ}^{ERS}	-1.61(0,89)	-1.53(0,89)	-1.89(0,89)	-4.20(5,85)[d]
$t_{\rho^*}^{ERS}$	-1.47(0,89)[a]	-0.21(4,87)	2.90(0,89)[d]	-
t_{ρ}	-	-	-	-

Table 1: The results of the ERS-tests for the German variables

	q_t	$u_t/\bar{y}_t$	$\bar{y}_t$	r_t
t_{ρ}^{ERS}	-2.06(0,91)	-2.03(0,91)	-3.42(7,84)[c]	-2.25(3,87)
$t_{\rho^*}^{ERS}$	-1.88(0,91)[a]	-0.40(0,91)	-	-1.39(3,87)
t_{ρ}	-	-	-	-1.79(4,86)[a]

Table 2: The results of the ERS-tests for the British variables

	q_t	$u_t/\bar{y}_t$	$\bar{y}_t$	r_t
t_{ρ}^{ERS}	-2.27(1,90)	-1.69(9,82)	-1.67(8,83)	-2.45(8,82)
$t_{\rho^*}^{ERS}$	0.38(0,91)	-0.74(9,82)	-0.72(8,83)	-1.62(8,82)[a]
t_{ρ}	-	-	-	-

Table 3: The results of the ERS-tests for the Japanese variables

	$u_t/\bar{y}_t$	$\bar{y}_t$	r_t
t_{ρ}^{ERS}	-2.39(3,88)	-9.48(1,90)[d]	-1.70(3,87)
$t_{\rho^*}^{ERS}$	-0.13(3,88)	-	-1.53(3,87)
t_{ρ}	-	-	-1.34(7,83)

Table 4: The results of the ERS-tests for the US variables

A lagged difference of the real yen/dollar exchange was added to the regression equation for the model with time trend. This was not done for the model with constant. Thus, according to the Beveridge-Nelson decomposition, the real yen/dollar exchange rate could contain a transitory component or not, that is, the real yen/dollar exchange rate could be a random walk or not. In summary, the evidence for the intertemporal equilibrium foreign exchange theory with flexible prices seems to be rather weak because two of the investigated real exchange rates are stationary around a constant and the third could have a transitory component. According to the test results, the mark/dollar and pound/dollar real exchange rates should be modelled as stationary variables with a constant in future real exchange rate models. The yen/dollar real exchange should be modelled as an I(1) process with a constant or with a time trend.

Because every model for one real exchange rate contains I(1) and I(0) variables, a cointegration procedure is needed which allows for both types of variables. The maximum likelihood procedure of Johansen is such a procedure. The results of the unit root tests also indicated that the German short-run real interest rate, the British and US GDP were trend-stationary. Thus an error correction model (=ECM) should be used which also allows for trend-stationary variables. In other words, the case of stochastic cointegration is relevant here[3]. It implies trending cointegrating residuals. However, the factor model of Gonzalo und Granger (1995) does not allow for trending cointegrating residuals. They have to be covariance-stationary in their model. Therefore, the author applied the ECM of Johansen (1991). This ECM just allows for time trends in the I(1) processes. The other variables have to be covariance-stationary. Appendix 1 shows the estimation and tests results for the case of stochastic cointegration. As can be seen in this appendix, the case of stochastic cointegration was confirmed by one of the tests (see table 38 in appendix 1). Campbell and Perron (1993, p. 781–784) showed with a trivariate VAR that the cointegration tests can underestimate the true cointegration rank when the ECM with deterministic cointegration is assumed although the ECM with stochastic cointegration is the data generating model. Campbell and Perron (1993) also illustrated that the application of the wrong ECM might also yield misleading inference about causality relations in the ECM[4]. Thus it seems dangerous to impose deterministic cointegration

---

[3]See for this case Johansen (1994a).

[4]Causality is meant in the sense of Granger causality.

although stochastic cointegration holds. On the other hand, the cointegrating residuals of the accepted cointegrating vectors for the case of stochastic cointegration do not look trending (see figures 11 to 13 in appendix 1). So it is still interesting to assume an ECM with deterministic cointegration. This is done in the next section. In addition, appendix 1 applies the tests from section D. to the case of stochastic cointegration. As can be seen in appendix 1, the test results from section D. hold for the case of stochastic cointegration too.

D. The Cointegration Analysis for the Case of Deterministic Cointegration and Tests with Respect to the Parameters of the Error Correction Model

To do the cointegration analysis the number of lagged differences k - 1 = k_1 in the ECM

$$\Delta X_t = \mu_0 + \alpha\beta' X_{t-1} + \sum_{i=1}^{k-1} \Gamma_i \Delta X_{t-i} + \Phi D_t + \epsilon_t. \tag{1}$$

has to be determined. α is the pxr adjustment matrix, β the pxr matrix of cointegrating vectors, and D_t is a 3x1 vector of centered seasonal dummy variables. Γ_i is a pxp matrix and Φ a px3 matrix. r is the number of cointegrating vectors. X_t is defined as: $X_t \equiv (q_t, \bar{y}_t, \bar{y}_t^*, u_t - \bar{y}_t, u_t^* - \bar{y}_t^*, r_t, r_t^*)$. Johansen and Juselius (1990) used the reparametrized VAR (vector-autoregressive system) (1) to determine the number of lagged differences for the ECM. They chose the number of lagged differences so that the errors were white noise processes in as many equations as possible according to the Box-Pierce Q statistics. The author applied this procedure to the three systems. Instead of using the Box-Pierce Q statistics he used the Box-Ljung Q statistics. They are supposed to have better size properties in finite samples. For the mark/dollar system k_1 was chosen to be 4, for the pound/dollar and yen/dollar system k_1 were assumed to be 2. Table 5 shows the Q statistics for the equations of the three ECM's for these numbers of lagged differences and for 15 and 22 autocorrelations. As can be seen from Table 5 not all equations (eq.) have white noise errors. However, it seems from the autocorrelations in tables 6 to 8 that most of them are spuriously significant[1]. The graphs of all residuals looked like residuals from white noise processes.

The errors of the three VARs showed also deviations from the normality assumption (see tables 9 to 12). The deviations in most equations were due to an excess kurtosis and ARCH[2] errors, respectively. Several simulation

---

[1]See, for example, the autocorrelation for lag 11 (0.302) for the third equation in the mark/dollar system (see table 6), the autocorrelation for lag 8 (-0.344) for the third equation in the pound/dollar system (see table 7) or the autocorrelation for lag 8 (-0.326) for the third equation in the yen/dollar system (see table 8).

[2]ARCH means autoregressive conditional heteroscedasticity.

eq.	Q(22) mark/$	Q(15) mark/$	Q(22) pound/$	Q(15) pound/$	Q(22) yen/$	Q(15) yen/$
1	28.762	21.358	21.030	14.125	26.375	19.090
2	16.039	8.233	18.816	12.004	14.720	9.508
3	30.372	23.826[a]	32.249[a]	25.541[b]	26.375	22.964[a]
4	17.996	12.316	19.855	15.861	17.540	14.333
5	13.308	9.017	32.073[a]	22.395[a]	26.640	16.069
6	15.611	11.778	26.183	15.082	17.087	8.761
7	25.678	15.193	38.693[c]	26.805[b]	30.490	18.073

Table 5: The Box-Ljung-Q-statistics for the mark/dollar, pound/dollar, and yen/dollar system

studies[3] investigated the effects of deviations from the normality assumption and, in addition, the effect of finite samples on the finite sample properties of the cointegration tests[4]. The simulation studies of Eitrheim (1992) and Cheung and Lai (1993) found that Johansen's cointegration tests might have size problems in finite samples under deviations from the normality assumption when these deviations are due to a high skewness and to ARCH errors with high ARCH coefficients. According to these simulation studies the values of skewness and ARCH(1) coefficients[5] that were found in this study should not cause large size distortions. However, it should be critically remarked that these simulation studies did not allow for time trends in the variables. Hence, the results of these simulation studies are only of limited use for this paper. An exception is Toda (1993, 1994). According to the knowledge of the author, he is the only one who investigated the properties (seize and power) of Johansen's cointegration tests for the case of deterministic and stochastic cointegration in finite samples but not under deviations under the normality assumption. He demonstrated that Johansen's cointegration tests might have power problems in finite samples[6]. Kostial (1994) showed that Johansen's

[3]See the Monte Carlo studies of Eitrheim (1992), Cheung and Lai (1993), Toda (1993, 1994), and Kostial (1994).

[4]These tests will be applied in the following.

[5]All of the estimated ARCH coefficients were below 0.4.

[6]He argues that the finite properties of Johansen's cointegration tests would have worsened further if there had been assumed deviations from the normality assumption.

1. eq.:	0.033	0.089	0.077	-0.043	-0.060	-0.288
	0.077	-0.204	-0.200	0.098	-0.102	0.054
	-0.075	0.051	0.217	0.022	0.108	0.049
	-0.066	0.050	0.012	-0.037		
2. eq:	-0.087	0.005	-0.025	-0.104	0.030	-0.037
	-0.043	-0.068	0.075	-0.106	0.001	-0.178
	-0.082	0.027	0.004	-0.085	-0.118	0.063
	0.135	-0.021	0.159	0.023		
3. eq.:	-0.119	-0.022	-0.042	-0.194	0.042	-0.051
	-0.075	-0.190	0.039	0.068	0.302	-0.203
	0.024	0.056	-0.155	0.158	-0.032	-0.025
	-0.087	0.027	-0.039	-0.001		
4. eq.:	0.016	0.110	0.019	-0.159	-0.009	-0.079
	-0.055	-0.100	-0.129	-0.006	-0.003	-0.140
	0.171	-0.054	-0.155	0.007	0.002	-0.039
	0.139	-0.033	0.074	-0.075		
5. eq.:	-0.072	-0.059	-0.064	-0.143	0.073	-0.089
	-0.067	-0.039	-0.059	0.150	0.058	-0.051
	0.084	0.046	-0.099	-0.088	-0.094	0.104
	-0.040	0.022	0.001	-0.122		
6. eq:	-0.154	0.046	-0.074	0.174	-0.135	-0.052
	-0.106	-0.009	0.070	-0.103	-0.049	-0.104
	0.042	0.021	-0.045	0.041	-0.028	-0.072
	0.068	-0.083	-0.112	0.001		
7. eq.:	-0.072	-0.018	-0.131	-0.005	-0.107	-0.106
	-0.217	0.185	0.019	0.028	-0.023	0.106
	0.076	0.109	-0.228	0.031	-0.060	-0.028
	-0.105	-0.103	0.127	0.130		

Table 6: The autocorrelations of the residuals for the mark/ dollar system with the confidence interval [-0.216, 0.216] for lags 1 – 22

1.eq.:	0.020	-0.102	0.027	-0.118	-0.136	-0.037
	0.048	0.097	-0.093	-0.076	-0.056	-0.048
	-0.239	0.078	0.083	0.019	0.026	0.141
	0.125	-0.112	0.066	-0.116		
2. eq:	-0.001	-0.008	-0.030	-0.121	0.076	0.094
	-0.059	-0.244	-0.016	-0.027	-0.130	-0.052
	-0.060	-0.062	0.065	0.064	-0.074	-0.055
	0.192	-0.051	0.059	0.031		
3. eq.:	0.010	-0.051	-0.091	-0.044	0.004	-0.024
	-0.022	-0.344	0.188	0.141	0.103	-0.197
	-0.074	-0.107	-0.090	0.069	-0.117	0.143
	-0.047	0.074	0.071	0.041		
4. eq.:	-0.004	-0.051	-0.002	-0.066	0.146	-0.058
	0.153	-0.153	0.052	0.032	-0.241	-0.100
	0.055	-0.070	-0.142	-0.031	-0.109	0.027
	-0.047	-0.012	0.017	-0.003		
5. eq.:	-0.048	-0.122	0.170	-0.079	-0.158	0.117
	-0.005	-0.278	0.034	0.057	-0.119	-0.046
	-0.129	-0.149	0.057	-0.051	-0.076	0.132
	0.052	0.030	0.225	0.067		
6. eq:	0.043	-0.069	-0.034	-0.043	-0.212	-0.085
	0.130	-0.080	-0.007	0.108	-0.100	-0.197
	0.068	-0.036	-0.078	-0.084	0.233	0.003
	-0.081	0.111	-0.109	-0.174		
7. eq.:	-0.046	-0.112	-0.058	0.188	0.093	-0.062
	-0.293	0.202	-0.005	-0.055	-0.238	0.001
	0.074	0.118	-0.301	-0.064	-0.007	-0.050
	-0.016	-0.015	0.103	0.169		

Table 7: The autocorrelations of the residuals for the pound/dollar system with the confidence interval [-0.213, 0.213] for lags 1 – 22

1.eq.:	0.095	-0.026	0.092	0.027	-0.167	-0.274
	-0.037	-0.102	-0.159	-0.013	-0.081	0.014
	-0.163	0.048	-0.015	-0.033	0.061	0.081
	0.100	0.071	0.190	0.181		
2. eq:	-0.073	0.023	-0.072	0.092	-0.035	-0.035
	0.019	-0.145	0.069	-0.071	0.040	-0.198
	-0.022	-0.025	-0.177	-0.081	0.025	0.014
	-0.035	-0.072	0.046	0.163		
3. eq.:	0.009	-0.064	-0.031	0.004	0.035	0.073
	-0.092	-0.326	0.140	0.068	-0.008	-0.121
	-0.173	-0.177	-0.059	0.090	-0.014	-0.024
	-0.040	0.100	0.078	0.110		
4. eq.:	-0.017	-0.098	-0.171	-0.197	0.202	-0.026
	0.084	-0.143	-0.003	-0.045	0.014	-0.031
	0.014	0.001	-0.050	0.067	-0.055	0.033
	0.035	0.093	0.084	-0.072		
5. eq.:	-0.010	-0.153	0.121	0.072	-0.123	-0.016
	0.024	-0.286	-0.110	0.019	-0.018	-0.041
	-0.040	0.085	0.037	-0.023	0.002	0.243
	-0.063	-0.034	0.162	-0.059		
6. eq:	-0.076	-0.049	0.073	-0.136	0.028	-0.145
	-0.024	0.033	0.122	-0.057	-0.093	-0.076
	0.028	-0.032	-0.123	0.065	-0.038	0.124
	-0.068	-0.158	0.087	0.003		
7. eq.:	-0.028	-0.014	0.030	0.205	0.069	-0.091
	-0.163	0.105	-0.095	-0.101	-0.252	-0.001
	0.032	0.062	-0.279	-0.032	-0.026	-0.115
	-0.084	-0.038	0.106	0.025		

Table 8: The autocorrelations of the residuals for the yen/dollar system with the confidence interval [-0.213, 0.213] for lags 1 – 22

eq.	skewness	excess kurtosis	J.-B. test statistic
1	0.325	-0.219	1.020
2	0.121	0.596	2.168
3	0.056	1.382	7.482[c]
4	-0.627	0.787	9.542[d]
5	-0.054	0.179	0.966
6	0.427	0.161	3.132
7	0.047	-0.285	0.026

Table 9: Skewness, excess kurtosis and Jarque-Bera test statistics for the mark/dollar system

eq.	skewness	excess kurtosis	J.-B. test statistic
1	-0.030	0.284	0.313
2	0.850	2.754	41.986[d]
3	0.012	1.353	5.719[a]
4	-0.067	0.490	0.963
5	0.319	0.580	4.796[a]
6	-1.064	4.511	81.199[d]
7	-0.368	0.496	3.690

Table 10: Skewness, excess kurtosis and Jarque-Bera test statistics for the pound/dollar system

cointegration tests might underestimate the true cointegration rank in finite samples when the "noise" in the system is high. Therefore, it seems advisable to look at the graphs of the cointegrating residuals when the cointegration rank is determined. Gonzalo (1994) and Eitrheim (1992) explored the finite sample properties of the maximum likelihood estimators (ML estimators) of the ECM (α, β, Γ_i, i = 1, ..., k - 1) under deviations from the normality assumption. According to the results of these simulation studies, the results of the estimations seem tenable. Again these authors did not allow for time trends in the variables.

Next Johansen's cointegration tests were applied to the two-country monetary model from section B. To test for the number of cointegrating

eq.	skewness	excess kurtosis	J.-B. test statistic
1	-0.245	-0.172	0.930
2	-0.901	2.842	44.024[d]
3	-0.629	1.858	17.610[d]
4	-0.392	3.556	45.849[d]
5	-0.227	-0.243	2.243
6	-0.785	3.655	59.604[d]
7	0.024	-0.161	0.068

Table 11: Skewness, excess kurtosis and Jarque-Bera test statistics for the yen/dollar system

eq.	ARCH(1) mark/$	ARCH(4) mark/$	ARCH(1) pound/$	ARCH(4) pound/$	ARCH(1) yen/$	ARCH(4) yen/$
1	0.188	2.863	0.024	3.851	0.147	4.176
2	0.368	2.337	0.734	10.118[b]	0.105	12.221[d]
3	0.960	9.992[b]	0.035	2.063	0.734	3.191
4	5.108[c]	6.034	0.042	1.297	2.314	33.659[d]
5	0.022	8.569[a]	5.737[c]	7.256	0.221	1.795
6	1.338	1.505	8.260[d]	9.415[b]	0.000	5.774
7	2.768[a]	4.804	0.150	5.598	0.649	4.468

Table 12: The results for the tests for ARCH errors in the mark/dollar system, pound/dollar, and yen/dollar system

vectors Johansen (1992, p. 390) suggested starting with the null hypothesis r = 0 to get good size and power properties for the cointegration tests. If this null hypothesis is rejected, the null hypothesis r ≤ 1 should be tested. If this null hypothesis is accepted, one cointegrating vector should be taken over into the ECM. If this null hypothesis is rejected again, one should go over to the next higher null hypothesis, etc. Tables 13 to 15 present the results of Johansen's cointegration tests for the trace and maximal eigenvalue statistic (λ_{max}). The critical values are taken from table 1 in Osterwald-Lenum (1992, p. 468). For the mark/dollar system, the trace and maximal eigenvalue statistic have accepted the null hypothesis r ≤ 1 (see table 13). But since the graphs of the cointegrating residuals of the second to fifth cointegrating vector also look stationary the null hypothesis r ≤ 5 was accepted although the stationarity of the cointegrating residuals of the fifth cointegrating vector might be questioned (see figure 2). According to table 14 both test statistics accepted two cointegrating vectors for the pound/dollar system. Because the cointegrating residuals of the third and fourth cointegrating also appear stationary (see figure 3), four cointegrating vectors were chosen for this system. For the yen/dollar system, the null hypothesis r ≤ 3 was accepted since the cointegrating residuals of the third cointegrating vector can also be considered as stationary.

H(r)	trace statistic	λ_{max}	λ_i
r = 0	142.277[d]	56.571[d]	0.482
r ≤ 1	85.706	27.586	0.274
r ≤ 2	58.120	24.798	0.250
r ≤ 3	33.322	18.854	0.197
r ≤ 4	14.468	10.029	0.110
r ≤ 5	4.439	3.779	0.043
r ≤ 6	0.659	0.659	0.008

Table 13: The values of the trace and maximal eigenvalue statistic for the mark/dollar system in the case of deterministic cointegration

H(r)	trace statistic	λ_{max}	λ_i
r = 0	153.052[d]	56.570[d]	0.474
r ≤ 1	96.482[b]	42.018[c]	0.380
r ≤ 2	54.464	27.128	0.265
r ≤ 3	27.337	14.177	0.149
r ≤ 4	13.159	8.409	0.091
r ≤ 5	4.751	4.728	0.052
r ≤ 6	0.023	0.023	0.000

Table 14: The values of the trace and maximal eigenvalue statistic for the pound/dollar system in the case of deterministic cointegration

H(r)	trace statistic	λ_{max}	λ_i
r = 0	150.259[d]	53.968[d]	0.458
r ≤ 1	96.291[b]	38.422[a]	0.354
r ≤ 2	57.869	26.996	0.264
r ≤ 3	30.873	14.737	0.154
r ≤ 4	16.136	11.474	0.122
r ≤ 5	4.662	4.124	0.046
r ≤ 6	0.538	0.538	0.006

Table 15: The values of the trace and maximal eigenvalue statistic for the yen/dollar system in the case of deterministic cointegration

Since rational speculative bubbles cause explosive exchange rate behavior, and the cointegrating residuals are covariance-stationary rational speculative bubbles can be excluded. Meese (1986, 365–369) was the first who tested for rational bubbles with the cointegrating technique of Engle and Granger (1987). A similar argument can be made for announced regime shifts for one or more fundamentals. Flood and Hodrick (1986, p. 837) have shown that these also imply an explosive exchange rate behavior. Similarly, exchange changes caused by learning processes can also be ruled out. Lewis (1988b) illustrates that the stochastic process for the conditional probability of a regime switch for one fundamental in the past is nonstationary. This process makes the stochastic process for the exchange rate nonstationary. But note that rational speculative bubbles do not have to exist when no cointegrating relations are found. The nonstationary behavior of real exchange rates could also be caused by announced regime shifts and learning processes, respectively. Flood and Hodrick (1986, p. 837–839) and Lewis (1988b, p. 13–14) pointed out these basic problems of tests for rational bubbles.

The ECM (1) assumes that at least one I(1) variable possesses a linear time trend. Since this assumption might be questioned, Johansen (1991, p. 1556) proposed a likelihood ratio test to test for it. The test statistic is asymptotically distributed as a χ^2 random variable with (p - r) degrees of freedom. Table 16 shows the results of this test for the three systems. The results confirm that at least one I(1) variable contains a linear time trend.

Johansen (1992) also constructed a test which allows testing for the cointegration rank and linear time trends simultanously. This test was not applied here since the proposed number of cointegrating vectors by the

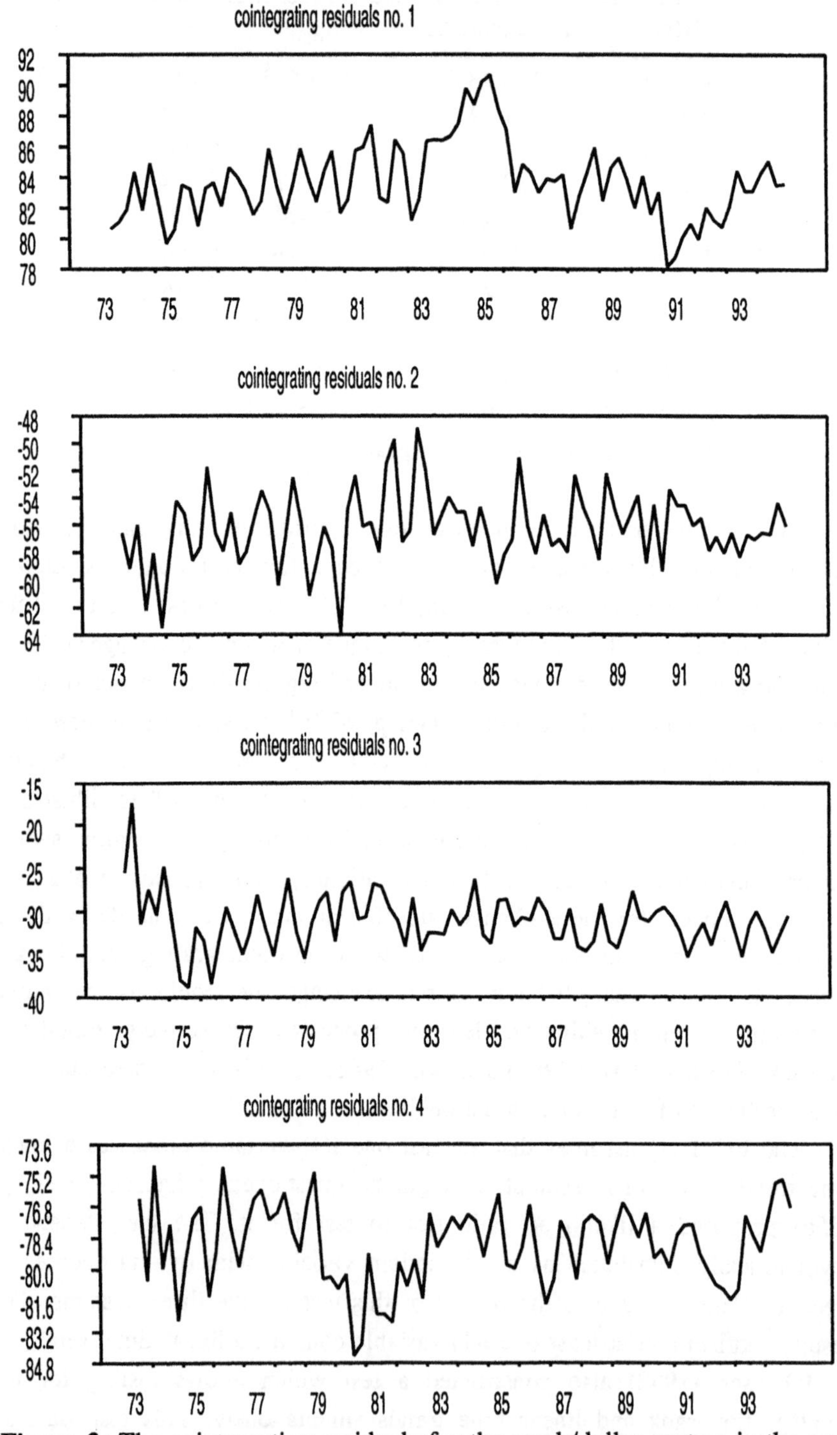

Figure 2: The cointegrating residuals for the mark/dollar system in the case of deterministic cointegration

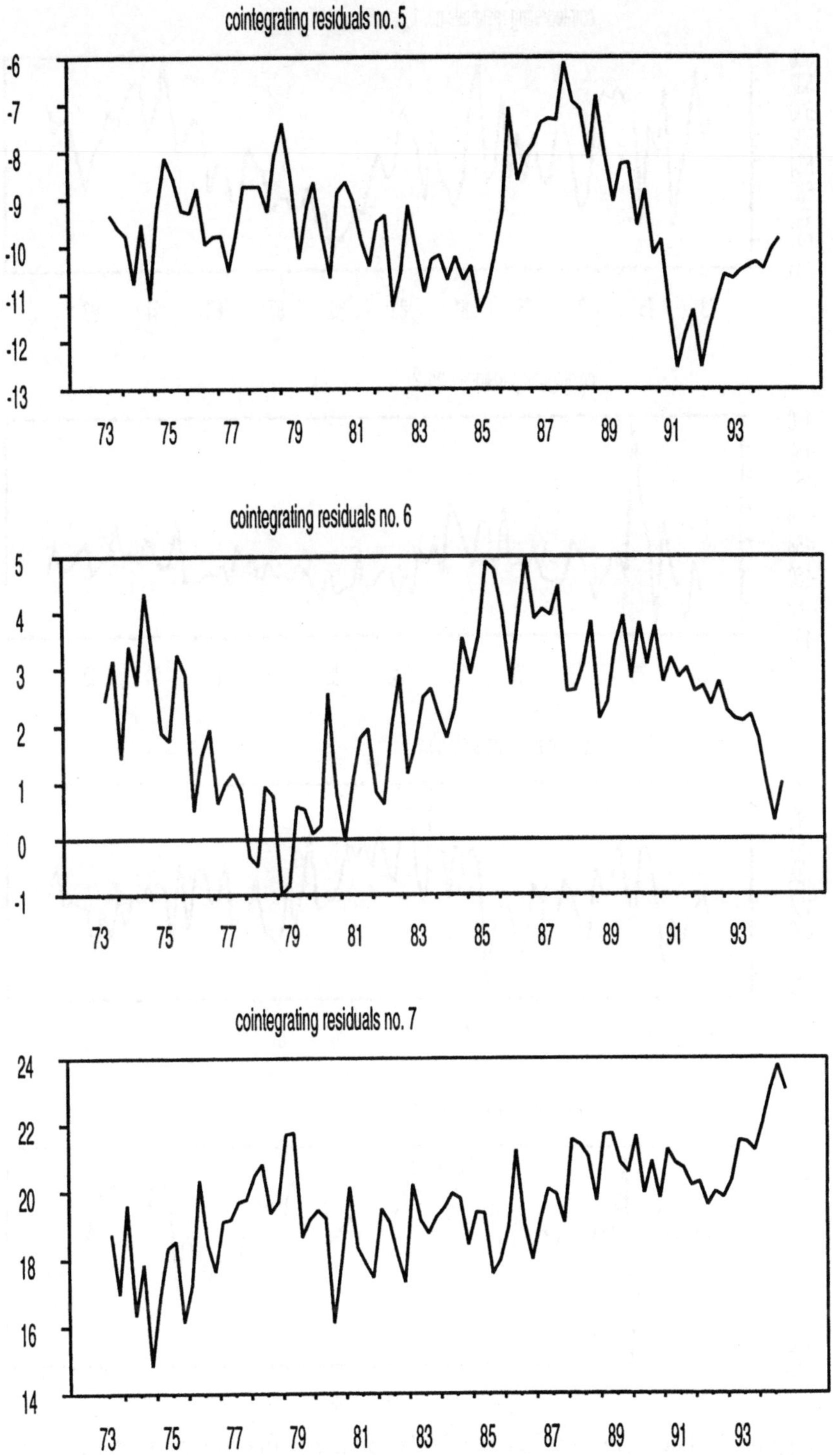

Continuation of figure 2

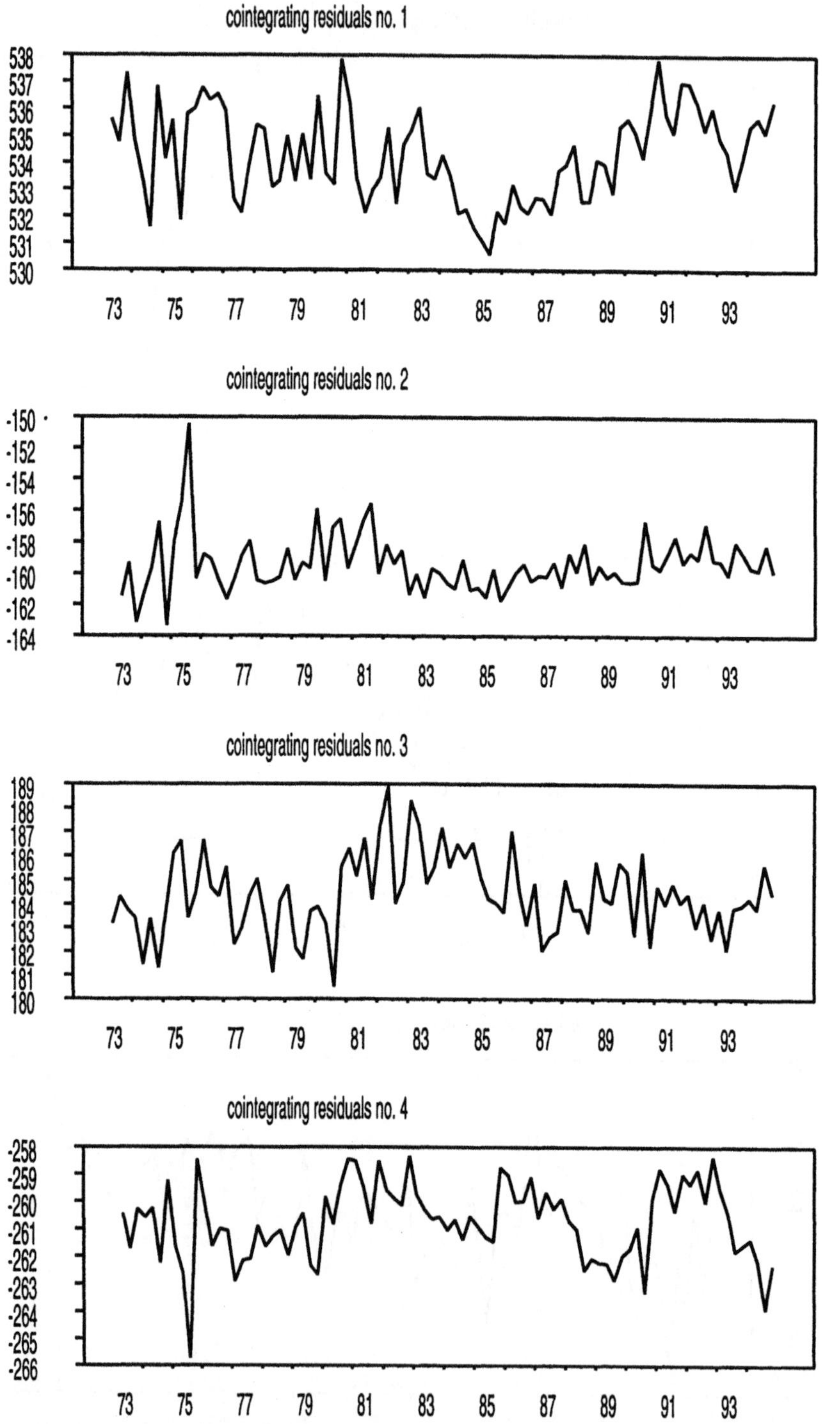

Figure 3: The cointegrating residuals for the pound/dollar system in the case of deterministic cointegration

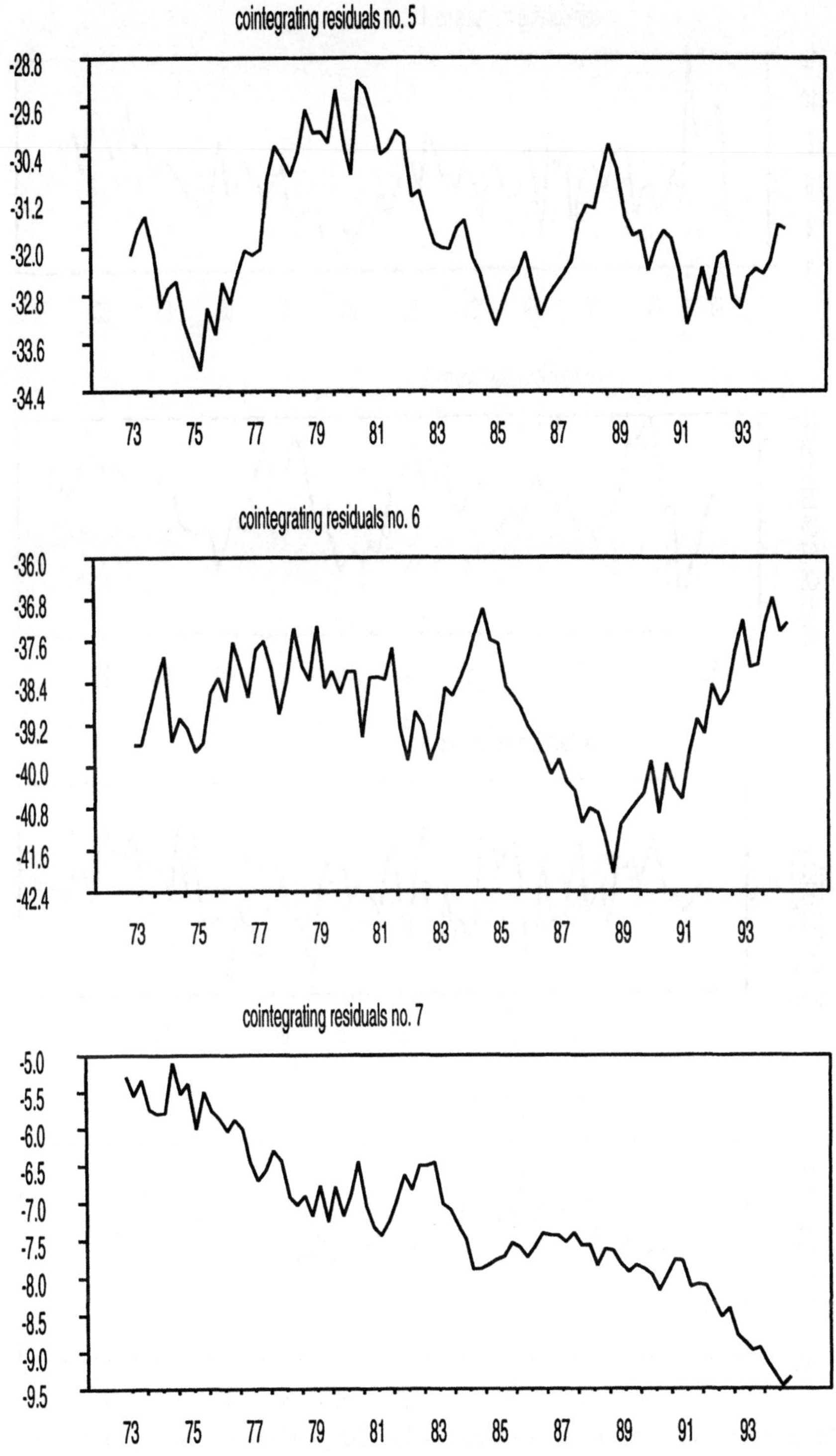

Continuation of figure 3

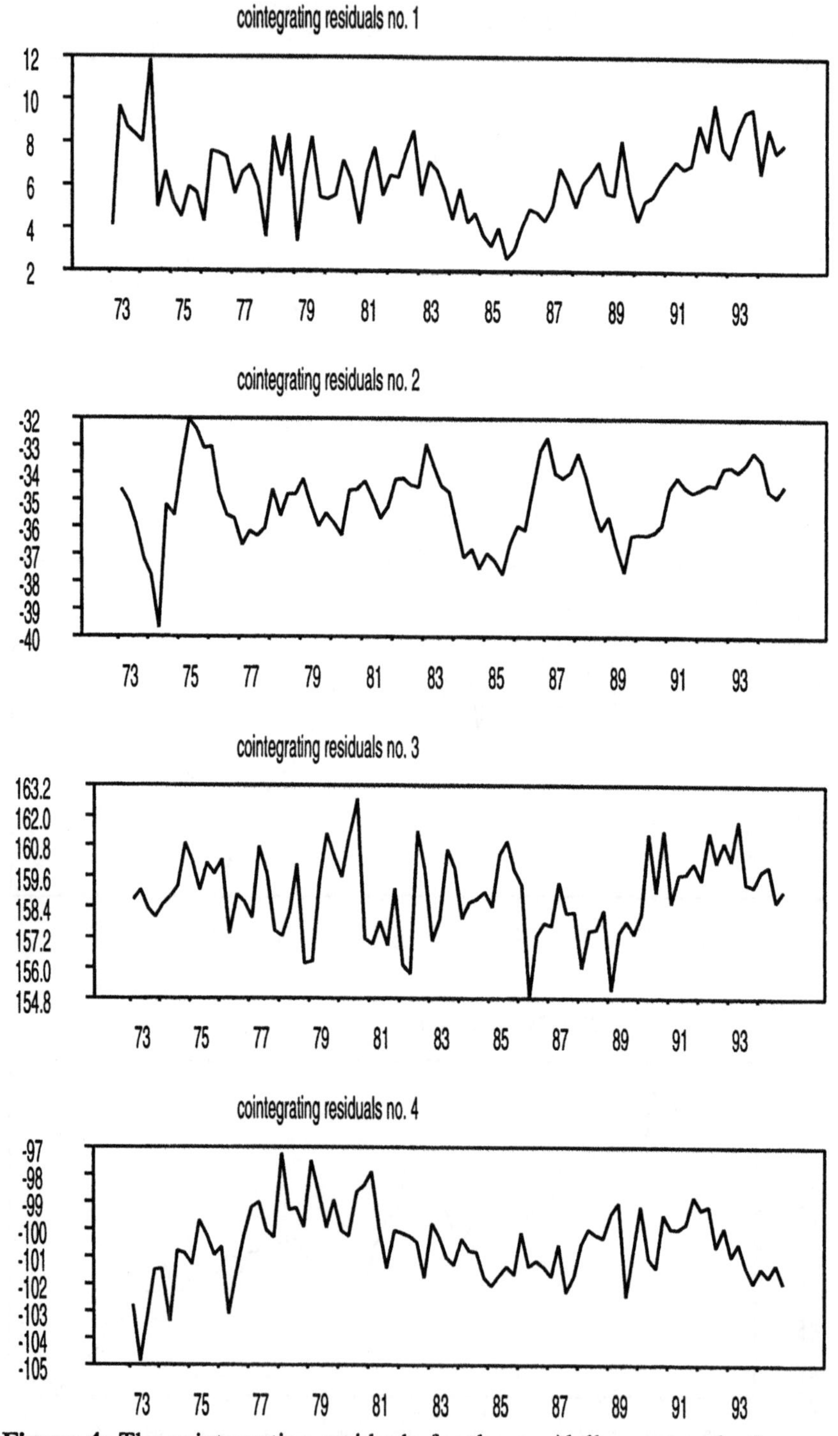

Figure 4: The cointegrating residuals for the yen/dollar system in the case of deterministic cointegration

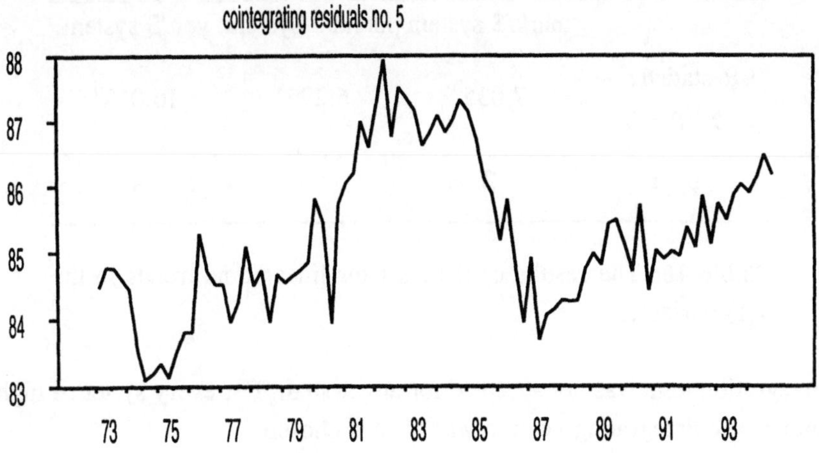

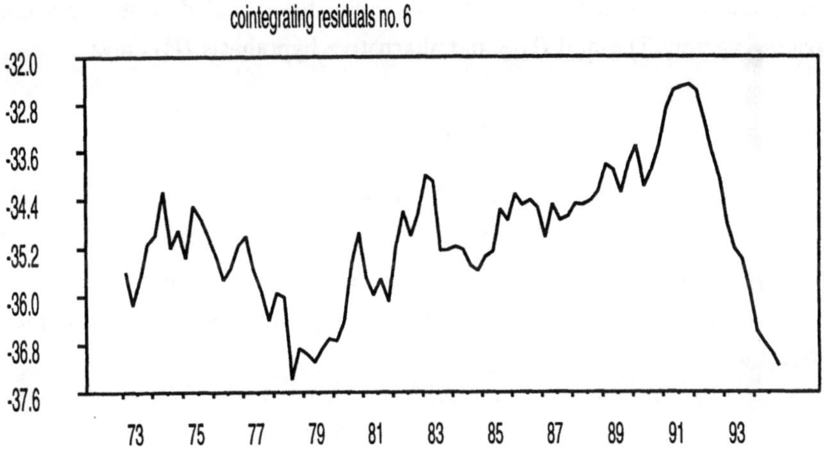

Continuation of figure 4

	mark/$ system	pound/$ system	yen/$ system
LR statistic ~ $\chi^2(p - r)$	7.035[b]	6.295[a]	16.018[d]
p - r	2	3	4

Table 16: The results of the tests for linear time trends in the I(1) variables

cointegration tests was not accepted for any system. For every system a higher number of cointegrating vectors was always chosen.

In a next step, tests were performed which allowed testing whether one cointegration parameter of one variable could be excluded from every cointegrating vector. The null (H_0) and alternative hypothesis (H_1) are:

(2)
$$H_0: \beta = H\varphi$$
$$H_1: \beta \text{ unrestricted}$$

where H is a pxs Matrix and φ a sxr matrix. s is equal to p minus the number of imposed restrictions on every cointegrating vector. For example, H is equal to

(3)
$$H_q = \begin{pmatrix} 0 & 0 & 0 & 0 & 0 & 0 \\ 1 & 0 & 0 & 0 & 0 & 0 \\ 0 & 1 & 0 & 0 & 0 & 0 \\ 0 & 0 & 1 & 0 & 0 & 0 \\ 0 & 0 & 0 & 1 & 0 & 0 \\ 0 & 0 & 0 & 0 & 1 & 0 \\ 0 & 0 & 0 & 0 & 0 & 1 \end{pmatrix}$$

if the cointegrating parameter of the real exchange rate is excluded from every cointegrating vector of one system. If the income variable of one system were excluded from one system, the second row of the matrix H would consist of zeros, etc. Johansen developed a likelihood ratio test to test this hypothesis. The likelihood ratio test statistic for this test is asymptotically distributed as a χ^2

random variable with r(p - s) degrees of freedom[1]. Johansen (1991, p. 1557) showed how to estimate φ. Since only one restriction is imposed on every cointegrating vector, s is equal to 6 here. The results in table 17 show that no variable could be excluded from all cointegrating relations of one system. Thus it seems that there are some long-run relationships among the variables of the two-country overshooting model from section B.

variable	mark/dollar system	pound/dollar system	yen/dollar system
q_t	38.092^d	28.469^d	14.185^d
$\bar{y}_t$	14.273^c	40.351^d	28.893^d
$\bar{y}_t^*$	10.725^a	38.560^d	19.570^d
$u_t - \bar{y}_t$	21.755^d	39.817^d	14.125^d
$u_t^* - \bar{y}_t^*$	30.972^d	22.599^d	13.627^d
r_t	20.006^d	29.469^d	28.189^d
r_t^*	27.187^d	19.701^d	11.502^d
r(p - s)	5	4	3

Table 17: The results of the tests for exclusion of a parameter of one variable from all cointegrating vectors in the case of deterministic cointegration

Furthermore, it was tested whether the adjustment parameters in the matrix α for the i-th equation are jointly zero. This is a test for weak exogeneity of a single variable. The null and alternative hypothesis of this test are:

$$\text{(4)} \qquad H_0\colon \alpha = A\psi \qquad H_1\colon \alpha \text{ unrestricted.}$$

where A is a pxm matrix and ψ a mxr matrix. m is equal to p minus the number of restrictions imposed on every vector in the matrix α. A is similarly

[1]For the likelihood ratio test statistic see Johansen (1991, p. 1558).

constructed as H. Johansen (1991, p. 1558) constructed a likelihood ratio test to test this kind of hypothesis. The likelihood ratio test statistic has asymptotically a χ^2 distribution with r(p - m) degrees of freedom. m is equal to 6 in this paper because only one restriction was imposed on every vector in the adjustment matrix α.

Table 18 presents the results of these tests for all equations for each system. In the mark/dollar system, the German short-run real interest rate is weakly exogenous (see eq. 6). In the pound/dollar system, US real GDP (see eq. 3) and the British real government expenditure-GDP ratio (see eq. 4) are weakly exogenous. The yen/dollar system has two weakly exogenous variables: The Japanese real government expenditure-GDP ratio (see eq. 4) and the US short-run real interest rate (see eq. 7). The three real exchange rates were not weakly exogenous.

eq.	mark/dollar system	pound/dollar system	yen/dollar system
1. eq.	11.255^{b}	15.728^{d}	16.156^{d}
2. eq.	10.897^{a}	18.147^{d}	16.563^{d}
3. eq.	12.218^{b}	4.918	8.531^{b}
4. eq.	12.158^{b}	6.361	1.710
5. eq.	24.984^{d}	13.753^{d}	25.382^{d}
6. eq.	1.365	29.864^{d}	11.439^{d}
7. eq.	15.789^{d}	8.879^{a}	3.958
r(p - m)	5	4	3

Table 18: The results of the tests for weak exogeneity of a single variable in the case of deterministic cointegration

Because no variable could be excluded from the cointegrating relationships and no real exchange rate is weakly exogenous, the fundamentals of all two country overshooting models have at least some transitory effects on the corresponding real exchange rates. Especially, monetary and fiscal policy had at least transitory effects on real exchange rates via short-run real interest rates and government expenditure-output ratios. They should be taken into account when monetary and fiscal policy measures are designed to stabilize real output and to control inflation. To quantify the effects of fundamentals on real exchange rates an impulse-response analysis would be required. Lütkepohl and Reimers (1992) showed how to perform impulse-response analyses in cointegrated systems.

In a further step, likelihood ratio tests were performed with respect to trivial cointegrating vectors (unit vectors) for the three real exchange rates. These cointegrating vectors have a one at their first components. If a trivial cointegrating vector were found for one real exchange rate, this real exchange rate would be covariance-stationary. That is, the null hypothesis of this test is covariance-stationarity of the considered real exchange rate. The alternative is that the considered real exchange rate is a I(1) process. The likelihood ratio test statistic for this test possesses asymptotically a χ^2 distribution with $(p - r)r_1$ degrees of freedom[7]. r_1 is the number of known cointegrating vectors. Here the test is related to one known or trivial cointegrating vector. Hence, r_1 is equal to 1 in this paper. Table 19 contains the results for these tests for the three real exchange rates.

The results show that all real exchange rates are I(1) processes. This is contrary to the results of the ERS-test for the real mark/dollar and pound/dollar exchange rate. The tests for trivial cointegrating vectors might be superior to the unit root tests since they take place in a multivariate framework. So they use more information. On the other hand, nothing is known about the finite sample properties of these tests, especially, when there are deviations from the normality assumption.

Finally, the significance of the parameters in the matrices $\alpha\beta' = \Pi$, Φ and Γ_i, $i = 1, \ldots, k - 1$ was checked. Lütkepohl and Reimers (1992, p. 60) derived the asymptotic distribution for the ML estimators of these parameters. Because the ML estimators of these parameters are asymptotically normally distributed, the usual t-tests can be used to test for significance of individual parameters. Tables 20 and 21 show the estimates of the parameters of the short-run dynamics for the real exchange rate equations. As is seen from these tables some of the fundamentals in each ECM have also some direct influence through the short-run dynamics on the real exchange rate. Particularly, changes in lagged differences of the US government-GDP ratio had short-run effects on all three real exchange rates (see table 21). Since the other equations also contained significant short-run dynamics parameters (not reported) some fundamentals, there are also indirect influences of the fundamentals

---

[7]For a derivation of this result see Johansen and Juselius (1992, p. 229). They also showed how the parameters of the ECM are estimated under the assumption of known cointegrating vectors.

	mark/dollar system	pound/dollar system	yen/dollar system
LR-statistic ~ $\chi^2[(p - r)r_1]$	4.695[a]	7.952[b]	23.955[d]
$(p - r)r_1$	2	3	4

Table 19: The results of the tests for trivial cointegrating vectors with respect to the three real exchange rates in the case of deterministic cointegration

on real exchange rates through the interactions in each ECM. Of course, the parameters of the short-run dynamics can not be used to quantify the effects of a change of a fundamental on a real exchange rate since the ECM is an interactive system. It has been already noted that an impulse-response analysis would be necessary to do this.

variable	mark/dollar system	pound/dollar system	yen/dollar system
q_{t-1}	-0.269[d]	-0.154[d]	-0.265[d]
$\bar{y}_{t-1}$	-0.005	0.346	0.453[c]
$\bar{y}^*_{t-1}$	-0.054	0.141	-0.874[d]
$u_{t-1} - \bar{y}_{t-1}$	-0.125	0.600[d]	0.152
$u^*_{t-1} - \bar{y}^*_{t-1}$	0.398[b]	0.052	0.131
r_{t-1}	0.000	-0.007	-0.030[d]
r^*_{t-1}	0.054[c]	0.044[d]	0.043[d]

Table 20: The results for the tests of significance of the parameters in Π for the equation of the real exchange rate in all three ECMs (deterministic cointegration)

Table 21: The results for the tests of significance of the parameters in Γ_i, i = 1, ..., k - 1, and Φ for the equation of the real exchange rate in all three ECMs (deterministic cointegration)

variable	mark/$ system	pound/$ system	yen/$ system
Δq_{t-1}	0.380^d	0.253^c	0.325^d
Δq_{t-2}	-0.020	0.292^d	0.087
Δq_{t-3}	0.242^c		
Δq_{t-4}	0.130		
$\Delta \bar{y}_{t-1}$	-1.673^c	-0.481	-0.285
$\Delta \bar{y}_{t-2}$	-0.129	0.444	1.352^b
$\Delta \bar{y}_{t-3}$	1.443^c		
$\Delta \bar{y}_{t-4}$	-0.382		
$\Delta \bar{y}^*_{t-1}$	3.103^d	0.535	1.242
$\Delta \bar{y}^*_{t-2}$	-0.608	-0.094	0.246
$\Delta \bar{y}^*_{t-3}$	-1.007		
$\Delta \bar{y}^*_{t-4}$	1.030		
$\Delta(u_{t-1} - \bar{y}_{t-1})$	-0.611	-0.681	0.017
$\Delta(u_{t-2} - \bar{y}_{t-2})$	0.543	0.187	-0.442
$\Delta(u_{t-3} - \bar{y}_{t-3})$	1.213^c		
$\Delta(u_{t-4} - \bar{y}_{t-4})$	-0.054		
$\Delta(u^*_{t-1} - \bar{y}^*_{t-1})$	2.270^d	1.073	2.001^d
$\Delta(u^*_{t-2} - \bar{y}^*_{t-2})$	-0.544	-1.471^b	-0.500
$\Delta(u^*_{t-3} - \bar{y}^*_{t-3})$	-1.074		
$\Delta(u^*_{t-4} - \bar{y}^*_{t-4})$	-0.301		
Δr_{t-1}	0.005	-0.002	0.030^d
Δr_{t-2}	0.005	-0.001	0.029^d

variable	mark/$ system	pound/$ system	yen/$ system
Δr_{t-3}	-0.008		
Δr_{t-4}	0.017		
Δr^*_{t-1}	-0.023	-0.013	-0.011
Δr^*_{t-2}	0.005	-0.004	0.005
Δr^*_{t-3}	0.016		
Δr^*_{t-4}	-0.021		
D_{1t}	-0.003	-0.005	-0.017
D_{2t}	-0.001	-0.019	0.011
D_{3t}	-0.014	-0.005	0.026[d]

Continuation of table 21

E. Forecasting

To judge the quality of the overshooting model from section B. the forecasting results of this model were compared with the out-of-sample forecasting results of the naive random walk model. Since the exchange rate is probably driven by "news" and different causes for excessive exchange rate movements, one cannot expect to get good forecasting results for structural exchange rate models. Despite these theoretical considerations, the out-of-sample forecasting results of the structural models were considered disappointing because the structural models did not perform better than the simple random walk model. Especially Meese and Rogoff (1983ab, 1988) showed this for different versions of the monetary model. This paper tries to improve upon these results by estimating the modified monetary model from section B. with Johansen's ML procedure.

Tables 15 to 22 present the root mean square forecast errors (RMSE) with respect to the real exchange rate for the three error correction models from section D[1]. The mean error (MA) and the absolute mean error (MAE) were also given to see whether the considered model over- or underestimates systematically. If both measures are approximately equal with the same sign, the monetary model underestimates systematically. Then the forecast is often below the realized value. If both measures are approximately equal in absolute value but with opposite sign, the monetary model overestimates systematically. In this case, the forecast is frequently above the realized value. The difference between the mean error and the root mean square forecast error shows how heterogenous the forecast errors are. If they differ to a greater extent the forecast errors have more outliers. If both measures are more or less of the same seize, the forecast errors are also more or less of the same seize. The forecasting statistics were constructed as follows: The monetary model from section B. was initially estimated in error correction form for each real exchange rate using data up through the fourth quarter of 1988. Thus the first forecast period was the first quarter of 1989. The number of lags for each error correction model was the same as in section D. Forecasts were generated at h = 1 to h = 20 quarters using a multivariate version of Wold's chain rule of forecasting. Then the second quarter of 1989 was added to the sample, and the parameters for each model were reestimated again. Forecasts for h = 1 to

[1]The forecast error is defined as $X_{t+h} - f_{t+h}$, where X_{t+h} is the realized value and f_{t+h} the forecasted value for the forecast period t + h. h is the number of forecasting periods.

20 steps were generated again and the resulting forecast errors were added to the forecasts statistics mentioned above. N_h is the number of errors which was used in computing the forecast statistics. Theil's U is the ratio of the RMSE of the monetary model to the RMSE of the random walk model. A value of Theil's U that is smaller than 1 means that the monetary model in error correction form produced better forecasts for the real exchange rate than the simple random walk model.

The results in Table 22 and 23 show that the random walk model performed better in terms of forecasting accuracy than the monetary model for the mark/dollar system. The results were more favourable to the monetary model for the case with only cointegrating vector (see table 23). Better results were obtained for the mark/dollar real exchange rate when the forecasts were made for the differences of the real mark/dollar exchange rate (see tables 24 and 25). The monetary model for the pound/dollar system with five cointegrating vectors could also beat the random walk for some forecasting horizons (see tables 26 and 27)[2]. The ML estimator yielded the best out-of-sample forecast results for the yen/dollar real exchange rate (see tables 28 and 29)[3]. In some cases there is also some over- and underestimation.

Hutchison/Throop (1985) and Kaminsky (1988) were also able to beat the random walk with their models. In Kaminsky's two-country model the real exchange rate depends on real income variables of both countries, ratios of total wealth to real income of both countries, budget deficit-income ratios of both countries, and on real oil prices. Total wealth is related to domestic and foreign government bonds. For the model with the pound/dollar real exchange rate, she used British oil production instead of oil prices to capture the North Sea oil effect. She estimated the model with the two-step estimator of Engle and Granger (1987). Her model attained slightly better results than the random walk model for the dollar/mark real exchange rate. The forecasting results were much better than those for the random walk model when the two-step estimator of Engle and Granger (1987) was applied to the model for the mark/yen real exchange rate. Hutchison and Throop (1985, p. 38) used an effective dollar real exchange rate and could beat the random walk for the period first quarter 1982 to the period first quarter 1985. Expected structural

---

[2]The monetary model could also beat the random walk for the pound/dollar real exchange rate at forecasting horizons h = 6 to 9 for the case with two cointegrating vectors.

[3]The monetary model also achieved better forecasting results than the random walk model for several forecasting horizons when other numbers of cointegrating vectors were assumed.

budget deficits-income ratios, long-term real interest rates and risk premia are the explaining variables in their model. They estimated their model with OLS and Cochrane-Orcutt.

h	ME	MAE	RMSE	Theil's U	N_h
1	-0.019	0.072	0.086	1.505	24
2	-0.068	0.130	0.175	2.080	23
3	-0.128	0.167	0.253	2.990	22
4	-0.193	0.223	0.316	3.617	21
5	-0.249	0.282	0.392	3.897	20
6	-0.326	0.351	0.461	4.749	19
7	-0.402	0.414	0.545	7.093	18
8	-0.484	0.485	0.644	9.058	17
9	-0.568	0.575	0.753	9.015	16
10	-0.654	0.654	0.862	9.568	15
11	-0.727	0.727	0.989	10.023	14
12	-0.776	0.789	1.127	9.546	13
13	-0.802	0.828	1.254	9.835	12
14	-0.777	0.802	1.312	10.925	11
15	-0.508	0.526	0.715	6.952	10
16	-0.467	0.501	0.719	7.561	9
17	-0.349	0.384	0.561	5.772	8
18	-0.211	0.229	0.283	2.743	7
19	-0.153	0.153	0.180	1.530	6
20	-0.140	0.160	0.182	1.277	5

Table 22: The forecasting results for the mark/dollar real exchange rate, k = 5, r = 5

h	ME	MAE	RMSE	Theil's U	N_h
1	-0.007	0.059	0.070	1.221	24
2	-0.028	0.088	0.115	1.360	23
3	-0.047	0.104	0.129	1.521	22
4	-0.059	0.129	0.151	1.732	21
5	-0.061	0.151	0.190	1.888	20
6	-0.069	0.150	0.187	1.926	19
7	-0.064	0.144	0.179	2.330	18
8	-0.064	0.175	0.206	2.898	17
9	-0.066	0.197	0.236	2.831	16
10	-0.065	0.197	0.225	2.497	15
11	-0.050	0.198	0.232	2.353	14
12	-0.031	0.228	0.263	2.227	13
13	-0.014	0.251	0.287	2.250	12
14	0.005	0.243	0.274	2.283	11
15	0.069	0.208	0.242	2.357	10
16	0.035	0.168	0.190	1.993	9
17	0.020	0.177	0.192	1.973	8
18	0.007	0.162	0.174	1.689	7
19	0.039	0.139	0.152	1.299	6
20	0.017	0.124	0.147	1.030	5

Table 23: The forecasting results for the mark/dollar real exchange rate, k = 5, r = 1

h	ME	MAE	RMSE	Theil's U	N_h
1	-0.019	0.072	0.086	1.062	24
2	-0.049	0.083	0.111	1.086	23
3	-0.059	0.081	0.108	1.371	22
4	-0.059	0.082	0.105	1.464	21
5	-0.051	0.077	0.108	1.076	20
6	-0.061	0.081	0.096	0.990	19
7	-0.061	0.096	0.114	1.853	18
8	-0.054	0.080	0.110	1.709	17
9	-0.053	0.084	0.109	1.123	16
10	-0.062	0.092	0.107	1.204	15
11	-0.063	0.103	0.136	2.133	14
12	-0.065	0.111	0.155	1.699	13
13	-0.074	0.121	0.168	1.633	12
14	-0.078	0.124	0.162	2.170	11
15	-0.038	0.084	0.101	2.304	10
16	-0.021	0.071	0.082	1.021	9
17	-0.013	0.043	0.050	0.712	8
18	-0.007	0.054	0.062	1.250	7
19	-0.001	0.051	0.058	1.135	6
20	0.003	0.053	0.059	0.609	5

Table 24: The forecasting results for the change in the mark/dollar real exchange rate, k = 5, r = 5

h	ME	MAE	RMSE	Theil's U	N_h
1	-0.007	0.059	0.070	0.862	24
2	-0.023	0.057	0.074	0.725	23
3	-0.021	0.055	0.071	0.905	22
4	-0.011	0.066	0.079	1.107	21
5	-0.006	0.066	0.079	0.781	20
6	-0.004	0.060	0.067	0.692	19
7	0.001	0.060	0.071	1.151	18
8	0.004	0.059	0.066	1.035	17
9	0.003	0.058	0.064	0.664	16
10	-0.002	0.052	0.060	0.675	15
11	-0.000	0.058	0.067	1.053	14
12	0.006	0.053	0.062	0.684	13
13	0.009	0.055	0.065	0.629	12
14	0.006	0.054	0.066	0.882	11
15	0.010	0.061	0.070	1.591	10
16	0.017	0.048	0.058	0.725	9
17	0.005	0.040	0.047	0.670	8
18	-0.004	0.041	0.050	1.005	7
19	0.001	0.044	0.052	1.011	6
20	0.006	0.047	0.053	0.553	5

Table 25: The forecasting results for the change in the mark/dollar real exchange rate, $k = 5$, $r = 1$

h	ME	MAE	RMSE	Theil's U	N_h
1	0.013	0.063	0.079	1.248	24
2	0.021	0.110	0.133	1.316	23
3	0.029	0.133	0.157	1.368	22
4	0.040	0.149	0.175	1.378	21
5	0.052	0.161	0.187	1.366	20
6	0.060	0.163	0.186	1.341	19
7	0.068	0.159	0.180	1.281	18
8	0.080	0.169	0.189	1.264	17
9	0.094	0.182	0.209	1.265	16
10	0.097	0.188	0.212	1.256	15
11	0.095	0.192	0.210	1.294	14
12	0.106	0.188	0.214	1.334	13
13	0.122	0.188	0.213	1.427	12
14	0.140	0.167	0.195	1.470	11
15	0.163	0.163	0.195	1.624	10
16	0.184	0.186	0.217	1.912	9
17	0.186	0.194	0.230	2.320	8
18	0.156	0.156	0.188	3.005	7
19	0.155	0.155	0.188	3.203	6
20	0.152	0.152	0.206	2.639	5

Table 26: The forecasting results for the pound/dollar real exchange rate, $k = 3$, $r = 4$

h	ME	MAE	RMSE	Theil's U	N_h
1	0.009	0.062	0.078	1.224	24
2	0.009	0.108	0.128	1.271	23
3	0.009	0.128	0.148	1.295	22
4	0.013	0.138	0.164	1.287	21
5	0.015	0.130	0.167	1.218	20
6	0.013	0.126	0.150	1.083	19
7	0.010	0.110	0.126	0.896	18
8	0.011	0.098	0.118	0.784	17
9	0.016	0.115	0.130	0.785	16
10	0.014	0.105	0.135	0.799	15
11	0.011	0.102	0.134	0.825	14
12	0.023	0.114	0.137	0.854	13
13	0.040	0.108	0.134	0.901	12
14	0.067	0.079	0.111	0.839	11
15	0.100	0.110	0.132	1.101	10
16	0.137	0.146	0.178	1.565	9
17	0.164	0.164	0.200	2.023	8
18	0.149	0.149	0.181	2.901	7
19	0.150	0.150	0.186	3.179	6
20	0.156	0.156	0.212	2.711	5

Table 27: The forecasting results for the pound/dollar real exchange rate, $k = 3$, $r = 5$

h	ME	MAE	RMSE	Theil's U	N_h
1	0.013	0.058	0.065	1.362	24
2	0.009	0.071	0.089	1.211	23
3	-0.000	0.080	0.099	1.206	22
4	-0.008	0.092	0.114	1.219	21
5	-0.009	0.118	0.143	1.260	20
6	-0.017	0.123	0.146	1.168	19
7	-0.022	0.116	0.135	1.035	18
8	-0.018	0.122	0.144	0.994	17
9	-0.013	0.130	0.155	0.966	16
10	-0.015	0.119	0.150	0.868	15
11	-0.008	0.102	0.129	0.707	14
12	0.001	0.098	0.116	0.590	13
13	0.008	0.088	0.107	0.496	12
14	0.003	0.072	0.088	0.396	11
15	0.005	0.084	0.097	0.423	10
16	0.007	0.081	0.097	0.402	9
17	-0.002	0.080	0.087	0.342	8
18	-0.021	0.054	0.061	0.235	7
19	-0.006	0.080	0.088	0.359	6
20	-0.017	0.081	0.090	0.399	5

Table 28: The forecasting results for the yen/dollar real exchange rate, k = 3, r = 3

h	ME	MAE	RMSE	Theil's U	N_h
1	0.020	0.053	0.062	1.298	24
2	0.023	0.070	0.082	1.118	23
3	0.022	0.064	0.087	1.060	22
4	0.022	0.067	0.098	1.048	21
5	0.026	0.095	0.127	1.118	20
6	0.021	0.100	0.127	1.015	19
7	0.015	0.101	0.118	0.898	18
8	0.013	0.116	0.132	0.910	17
9	0.008	0.131	0.154	0.959	16
10	-0.002	0.137	0.153	0.888	15
11	-0.002	0.117	0.132	0.722	14
12	-0.003	0.102	0.129	0.654	13
13	0.000	0.099	0.124	0.573	12
14	-0.008	0.082	0.111	0.501	11
15	-0.006	0.090	0.111	0.483	10
16	0.004	0.079	0.100	0.414	9
17	0.003	0.071	0.083	0.326	8
18	-0.012	0.046	0.055	0.211	7
19	-0.001	0.073	0.089	0.363	6
20	0.001	0.089	0.099	0.441	5

Table 29: The forecasting results for the yen/dollar real exchange rate, $k = 3$, $r = 4$

F. The Application of the Factor Model

Gonzalo's and Granger's decomposition of a cointegrated vector X_t into a permanent component ($A_1\alpha_\perp' X_t$) and transitory component ($A_2\beta' X_t$) is as follows:

(1) $$X_t = A_1\alpha_\perp' X_t + A_2\beta' X_t.$$

where $\alpha_\perp$ is the px(p-r) orthogonal matrix to α (for the definition of α see section D.). A_1 is a px(p-r) matrix and A_2 a pxr matrix. Gonzalo and Granger (1995, p. 28, 34) prove that $A_1\alpha_\perp' X_t$ is indeed a permanent component in the sense that innovations of it have a permanent effect on it. $A_2\beta' X_t$ is transitory per definition since the cointegrating residuals are covariance-stationary. $\alpha_\perp' X_t$ are the common trends (common long-memory components). They are identified in the above factor model up to a non singular transformation to the left[1]. Intuitively, they are the driving forces of the economy which are independent of the equilibrium errors. They move the components of X_t on the equilibrium hyperplane back and forth and cause changes of the variables in the long-run. This point can be explained with the help of figure 4 where a two-variable error correction model with no lagged differences is assumed. In the long-run, the equilibrium error $z_t = \beta' X_{1t}$ is equal to zero and X_{1t} and X_{2t} are on the straight line $X_{1t} = \beta' X_{2t}$. Because of the error correction model X_{1t} and X_{2t} are attracted by adjustment processes to this line. Therefore, this line is called attractor set in the literature. The direction of adjustment is determined by the adjustment vector α of the error correction model. The adjustment processes are triggered by shocks $\epsilon_{it} = i = 1, \ldots, p$ where ϵ_{it} is the i-th component of the vector ϵ_t with respect to variable i. The common trends $\alpha_\perp X_t$ determine the point on the equilibrium hyperplane ($X_{1t} = \beta X_{2t}$) to which the vector X_t moves in the long-run. They move the components of $X_t = (X_{1t}, X_{2t})$ on the hyperplane $X_{1t} = \beta X_{2t}$ line. Thus they generate the long-run relationship of X_{1t} and X_{2t} over time. The values on the permanent components of X_t are those which are realized on the hyperplane or the attractor set. Therefore, it makes sense to say that the realized values of a real exchange rate on its permanent component are the fundamental exchange

[1]For details about the identification problem with respect to the common trends, see Gonzalo and Granger, 1995, p. 27, 29.

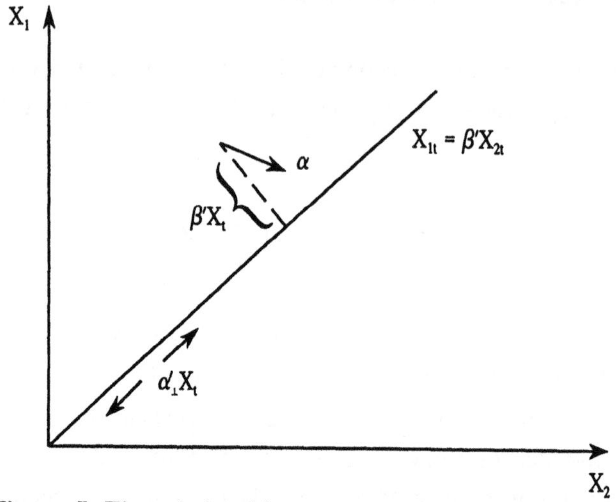

Figure 5: The relationship among attractor set, equilibrium error, and the common trends (Source: with slight modifications taken from Johansen, 1994b, p. 358)

rates although the real exchanges rate might have also been driven by real exchange rate innovations as can be seen from equation (1)[2].

As was mentioned in section A., the transitory component is interpreted to consist mainly of covariance-stationary excessive real exchange rate movements and of real exchange rate movements caused by "news".

Gonzalo and Granger (1995, p. 30) show[3] how to estimate the common trend matrix $\alpha_\perp$ and how to test null restrictions with respect to one particular parameter in every vector of $\alpha_\perp$. Because the parameters in $\alpha_\perp$ are not identified the estimates of these parameters are not reported.

Figure 6 presents the realized, real exchange rate development (solid line q), the estimated permanent component (dashed line P with the short dashes), and the estimated transitory component (dashed line T with the long dashes) for all three real exchange rates. As can be seen from the figures, the estimated transitory component for the pound/dollar system and the yen/dollar system is relatively large. The permanent component of the pound/dollar real exchange rate is greater than the permanent component of the yen/dollar system. The transitory component is smaller for the mark/dollar system.

---

[2]The vector X_t on the right-hand side in equation (1) contains also the real exchange rate.

[3]See also Johansen, 1995, p. 128-130.

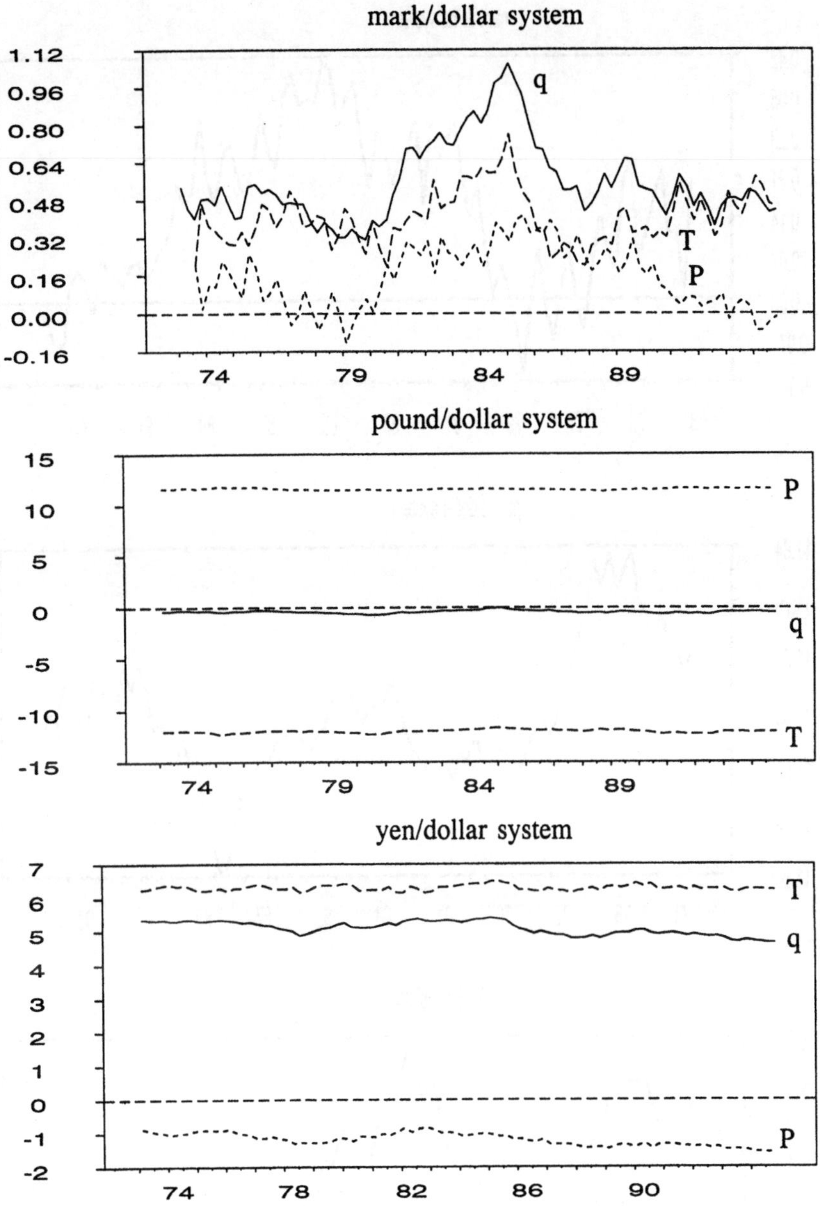

Figure 6: The realized real exchange rate development (line q), the estimated permanent component (line P), and the transitory component (line T) for the three real exchange rates

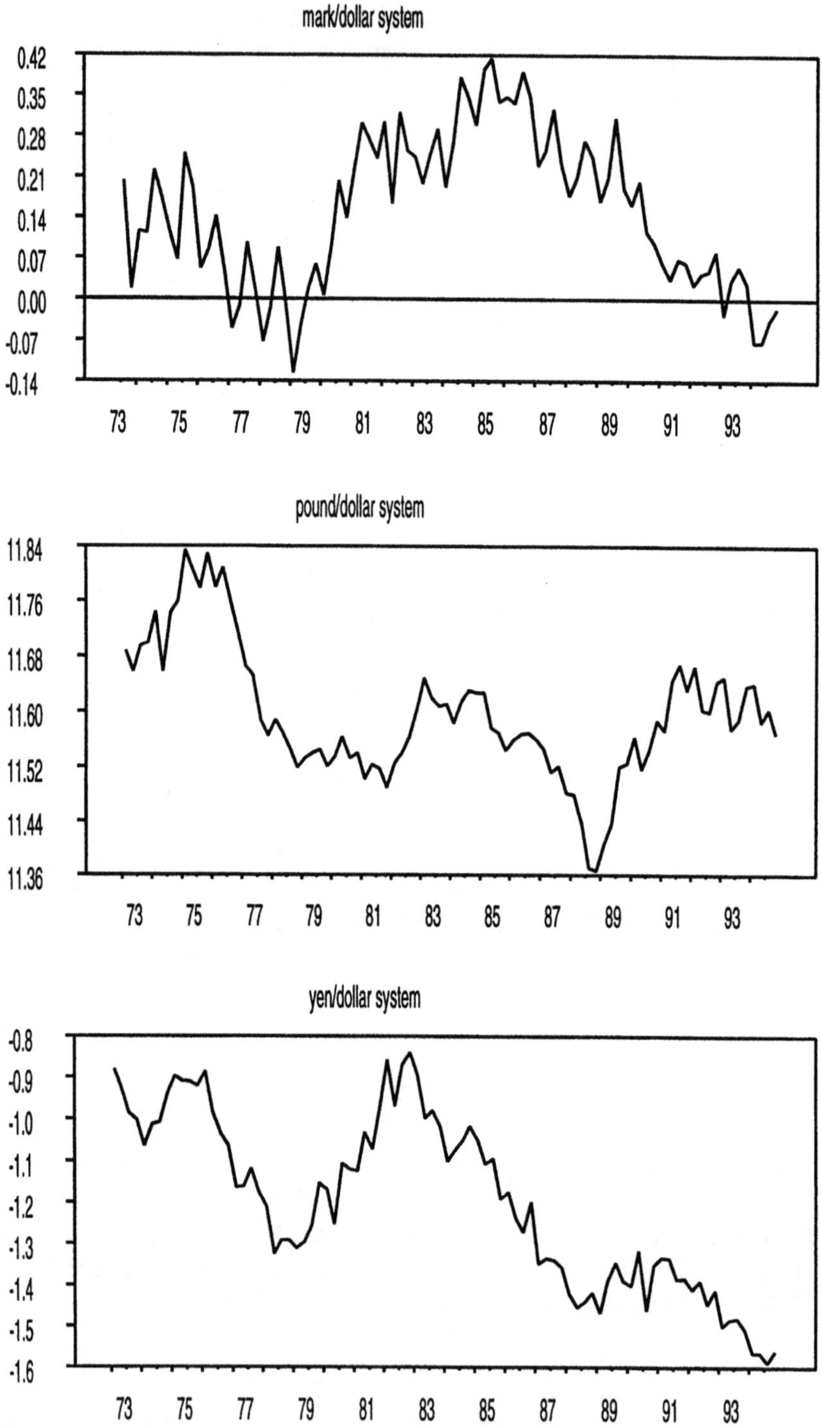

Figure 7: The time series of the estimated permanent components of the three real exchange rates

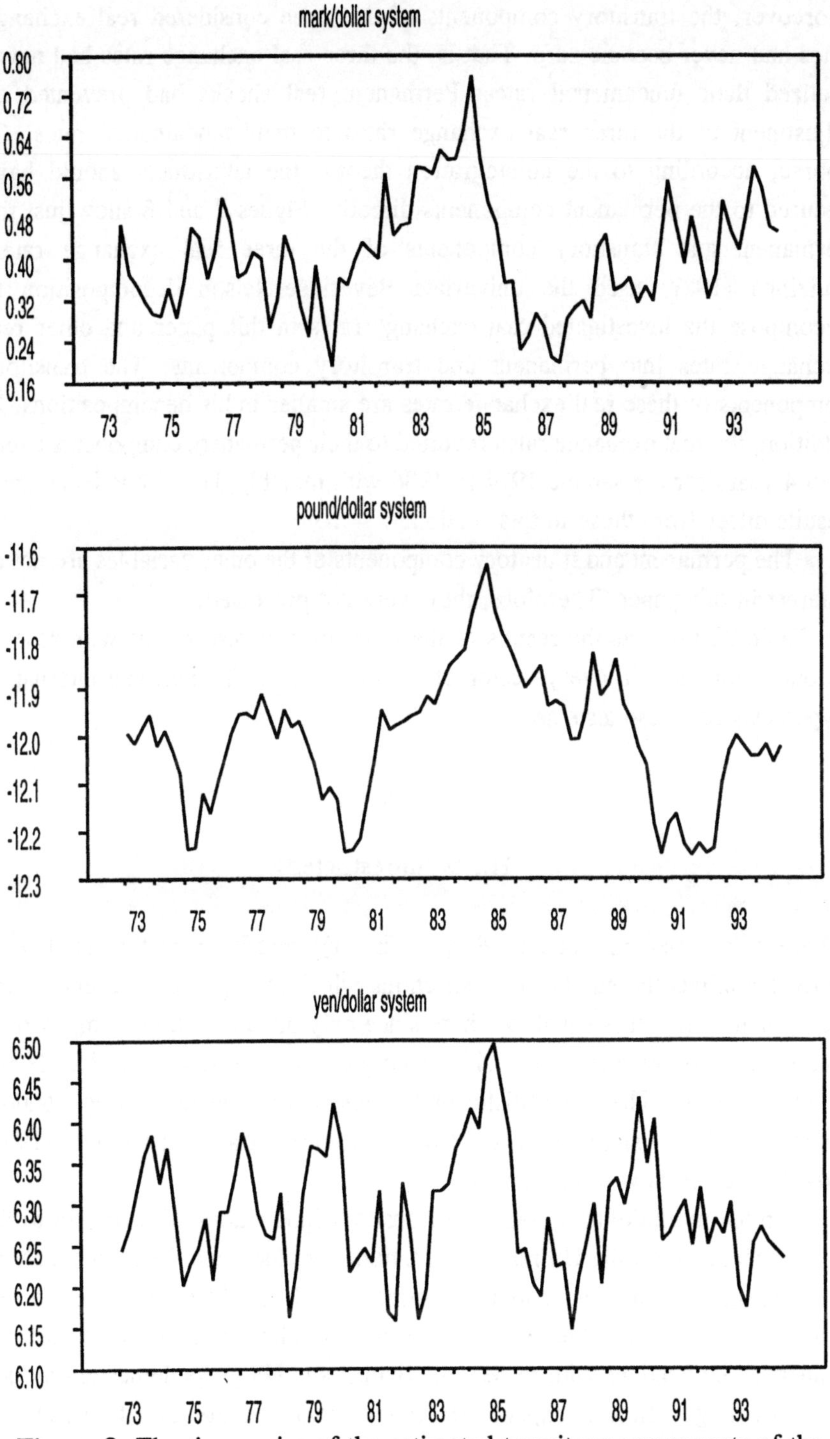

Figure 8: The time series of the estimated transitory components of the three real exchange rates

Moreover, the transitory components of the three considered real exchange rates had never become zero. That is, the three real exchange rates had never realized their fundamental rates. Permanent real shocks had prevented an adjustment of the three real exchange rates to their fundamental rates. Of course, according to the cointegration theory, the adjustment should have occured to the permanent components directly. Figues 7 and 8 show just the permanent and transitory components of the three real exchange rates. Huizinga (1987) used the univariate Beveridge-Nelson decomposition to decompose the investigated real exchange rates in this paper and other real exchange rates into permanent and transitory components. The transitory components of these real exchange rates are smaller in his decompositions. In addition, the real exchange rates reverted to their permanent components every 2 to 4 years for the sample 1974 to 1986 with monthly data. Thus Huizinga's results differ from those in this section.

The permanent and transitory components of the other variables are not of interest in this paper. Therefore, they were not presented.

Table 23 presents the results of the tests for null restrictions with respect to one component in every vector of the matrix $\alpha_{\perp}$. The null and alternative hypothesis for these tests are:

$$(2) \qquad \begin{aligned} &H_0: \alpha_{\perp} = J\theta \\ &H_1: \alpha_{\perp} \text{ unrestricted,} \end{aligned}$$

where J is a pxn matrix and θ a [nx(p - r)] matrix. n is the number of variables minus the number of restrictions which is imposed on every vector of the matrix $\alpha_{\perp}$. It is equal to 6 here since only one restriction is imposed on every vector of the matrix $\alpha_{\perp}$. J is similarly constructed as the matrices H and A in section D. The test statistic of this test is distributed as a χ^2 random variable with (p - r)x(p - n) degrees of freedom. Gonzalo and Granger (1995, 30–31) showed how to estimate θ.

In the mark/dollar system, the transitory innovations with respect to the real exchange rate, the US real gross national product, and the German short-run real interest rate had a long-run effect on all variables including the real exchange rate (see table 30). In the pound/dollar system, these are the transitory innovations with respect the British and US gross domestic product, the British government expenditure-output ratio and the US short-run real interest rate. Innovations with respect to the US gross domestic product, the

Japanese and US government expenditure-output ratio and with respect to the Japanese and US short-run real interest rate possessed a long-run effect on the yen/dollar real exchange rate and the other variables in the yen/dollar system.

variable	mark/$ system	pound/$ system	yen/dollar system
q_t	6.136^b	1.167	6.106
$\bar{y}_t$	0.180	6.239^a	6.576
$\bar{y}_t^*$	5.351^a	7.391^a	18.705^d
$u_t - \bar{y}_t$	2.384	9.369^c	17.829^d
$u_t^* - \bar{y}_t^*$	2.987	5.173	10.924^d
r_t	7.010^b	0.289	20.935^d
r_t^*	1.938	10.590^c	14.919^d
(p - r)x(p - m)	2	3	4

Table 30: The results of the tests with respect to null restrictions on $\alpha_\perp$

Provided that real income and fiscal shocks also had quantitatively sufficient effects on the three real exchange rates, the implementation of a system with limited exchange rate flexibility would be problematic. Section A. explained why this is true. Contrary to the argumentation in section A., only temporary real shocks are necessary to get permanent effects on real exchange rates. For the mark/dollar system there is also some long-run control possibility by German monetary policy over the mark/dollar real exchange via short-run real interest rates. US monetary policy could influence the pound/dollar real exchange rate through short-run real interest rates in the long-run and British fiscal policy could do that through changes in government expenditure. Some control possibilities also exist by Japanese and US monetary and fiscal policies on the yen/dollar real exchange rate in the long-run. To quantify the long-run effects of monetary and fiscal policies on the three real exchange rates an impulse-response analysis would be necessary. These results are interesting for the first subgroup in the first main group in section A. because monetary policy or monetary and fiscal policy, respectively, had some permanent effects on real exchanges rates in each system in the long-run.

Unfortunately, no simulation studies exist about the finite sample properties for the tests with respect to the matrix $\alpha_{\perp}$, especially under the assumption of non-normality. Since deviations from the normality assumption were found, these might be problematic for the test results.

To determine the effects of "news" with respect to fundamentals, innovations had to be constructed. The residuals of estimated autoregressive processes (AR processes) for one fundamental were taken to be the innovations of this fundamental[3]. To estimate the influence of "news" on changes in the transitory component of one real exchange rate (ΔTq_{it}), the following equations for the three real exchange rates were estimated with the Seemingly Unrelated Regression technique (=SUR technique)[4]:

$$
\begin{aligned}
\Delta Tq_{it} = {} & a_0 + a_1(\bar{y}_{it} - \bar{y}_{it}^{f}) + a_2(\bar{y}_t^{*} - \bar{y}_t^{*f}) + a_3[(u_{it} - \bar{y}_{it}) - (u_{it} - \bar{y}_{it})^{f}] \\
& + a_4[(u_t^{*} - \bar{y}_t^{*}) - (u_t^{*} - \bar{y}_t^{*})^{f}] + a_5(r_{it} - r_{it}^{f}) \\
& + a_6(r_t^{*} - r_t^{*f}) + \epsilon_{it}.
\end{aligned}
\tag{3}
$$

for i = 1, 2, 3. "f" means "forecast". Thus the variables marked with an "f" are the forecasts of the market based on estimated autoregressions. The differences on the right hand side of equation (1) are then the innovations ("news"). The symbol * describes US variables. Normally, "news" equations contain the first difference of the one-period lagged forward exchange rate to measure the influence of the expected change of the nominal exchange rate. In section A., it was explained why the expected change of the transitory component was not added to the regression equations. The SUR technique was used to avoid efficiency losses since the innovations of the three equations should be correlated because the considered countries should be hit to some extent by the same shocks[5].

---

[3]Frenkel (1981, p. 687) and Edwards (1982, p. 216) constructed innovations in this way.

[4]Changes in the transitory components were considered since the levels of the transitory components were not well explained by the innovations with respect to fundamentals. A constant explained a large part of the movement of the three transitory components.

[5]Edwards (1982) showed this correlation theoretically with a monetary multi-country

According to the instructions of Granger and Newbold (1986, p. 83), the number of lags for the AR processes was determined with the BIC. A constant was included in the autoregressive processes when the fundamental was an I(1) process according the unit tests from section C. The constant implies a time trend for these variables. For the British and US domestic gross national product the autoregressions contained a time trend since the unit root test by ERS considered these variables as trending with a time trend. For all real interest rates an autoregressive model with a constant was chosen because some of the interest rates were I(0) variables or looked stationary around a constant according to their graphs[6]. Table 31 contains the assumed number of lags for the autoregressive models for the different variables. To get white noise residuals a higher number of lags was used for some variables than that proposed by the BIC. C means that a model with constant was used. "tre" stands for "trend" and means that the estimated model contained a time trend and a constant. Since the eighth and twelfth autocorrelation were significant for the AR process of the US GDP, the Q statistics with 15 and 22 autocorrelations got also significant at a significance level of one percent. The significant autocorrelations were considered accidental. The residuals of the AR processes of the other variables were white noise processes at usual significant levels according to the Ljung-Box Q statistics.

The estimated variance covariance matrix of the SUR residuals was multiplied by the factor 1/(T - 7) so that the estimators of the variances and covariances became unbiased[7]. It was just iterated once.

According to the results of Pagan (1984, p. 233), the generated regressors should have no negative consequences for the efficiency of the estimators since the regression equations contained a constant[8]. Also, the t statistics are asymptotically appropriate to test for significance of the parameters since the

---

model.

[6]This specification is in contrast to the results of the unit root tests for the German and US short-run real interest rate in section C. The German short-run real interest rate was considered trend-stationary, the US short-run real interest rate was a I(1) process. But according to the graph of the German real interest rate it seemed to be better represented by a an autoregressive model with a constant. The US short-run real interest rate looked more like a stationary variable around a constant although it could have had a structural break (upward shift) around 1980. This might have impaired the power of the ERS unit root test.

[7]T means sample size here.

[8]More precisely Pagan (1984, p. 233) showed this only for the OLS method.

	GER	UK	JP	US
$u_t - \bar{y}_t$	5, C	1, C	3, C	4, C
$\bar{y}_t$	1, C	5, tre	9, C	2, tre
r_t	8, C	5, C	8, C	4, C

Table 31: The chosen models and lag lengths for the AR(k)-processes of fundamentals

variance covariance matrix is still valid[9]. But it is not known which effects the generated regressand does have on the SUR estimator and its variance covariance matrix.

Table 32 contains the results of the SUR estimation. The sample is from the second quarter 1974 to the fourth quarter 1994. "g" stands for $u_t - \bar{y}_t$ and designates the ratio government expenditure output-ratio. In every system, some variables have the right sign. However, the Q statistics for 13 and 20 autocorrelations are significant for the mark/dollar and pound/dollar system at usual significance levels. Although the Q statistics for the yen/dollar were not significant, the first, fourth, eleventh, fifteenth, and sixteenth autocorrelation came very close to the upper bound. These results indicate that the residuals of this system are not white noise either. Thus the t statistics are not useful to test for significance. It would have been possible to estimate the SUR system again with quasi differences of the innovations. This was not done since the transformed innovations do not make sense from an economics view. The autocorrelated errors in each equation show that the innovations of the different fundamentals were not able to explain the changes of the transitory components very well. This impression is confirmed by the fit of the estimated SUR system in figure 9.

Table 33 shows the correlations between the residuals of the different equations of the SUR system. Since these autocorrelations are of some value, it made sense to apply the SUR technique.

Because the usual coefficient of determination is not between 0 and 1 for one equation of a SUR system, the coefficient of determination by McElroy

[9]Pagan (1984, p. 233) showed this for the OLS method.

	$\Delta Tq_{mark/\$}$	$\Delta Tq_{pound/\$}$	$\Delta Tq_{yen/\$}$
Constant	-0.001	-0.001	0.000
$\bar{y}_t - \bar{y}_t^f$	0.622	-1.857[d]	0.492
$\bar{y}_t^* - \bar{y}_t^{*f}$	-1.324	0.763	1.038
$g_t - g_t^f$	-1.790[d]	-2.163[d]	-1.0048[d]
$g_t^* - g_t^{*f}$	-1.894[c]	-1.271[b]	-1.820[d]
$r_t - r_t^f$	-0.081[d]	0.008[a]	0.012[a]
$r_t^* - r_t^{*f}$	-0.002	0.013	-0.072[d]
R_*^2		0.546	
Q(13)	58.904[d]	24.525[b]	16.345
Q(20)	66.232[d]	36.066[c]	24.879

Table 32: The results of the SUR estimation

	mark/$ system	pound/$ system	yen/$ system
mark/$ system	1.000		
pound/$ system	0.355	1.000	
yen/$ system	0.650	0.484	1.000

Table 33: The estimated correlation matrix for the residuals of the SUR model

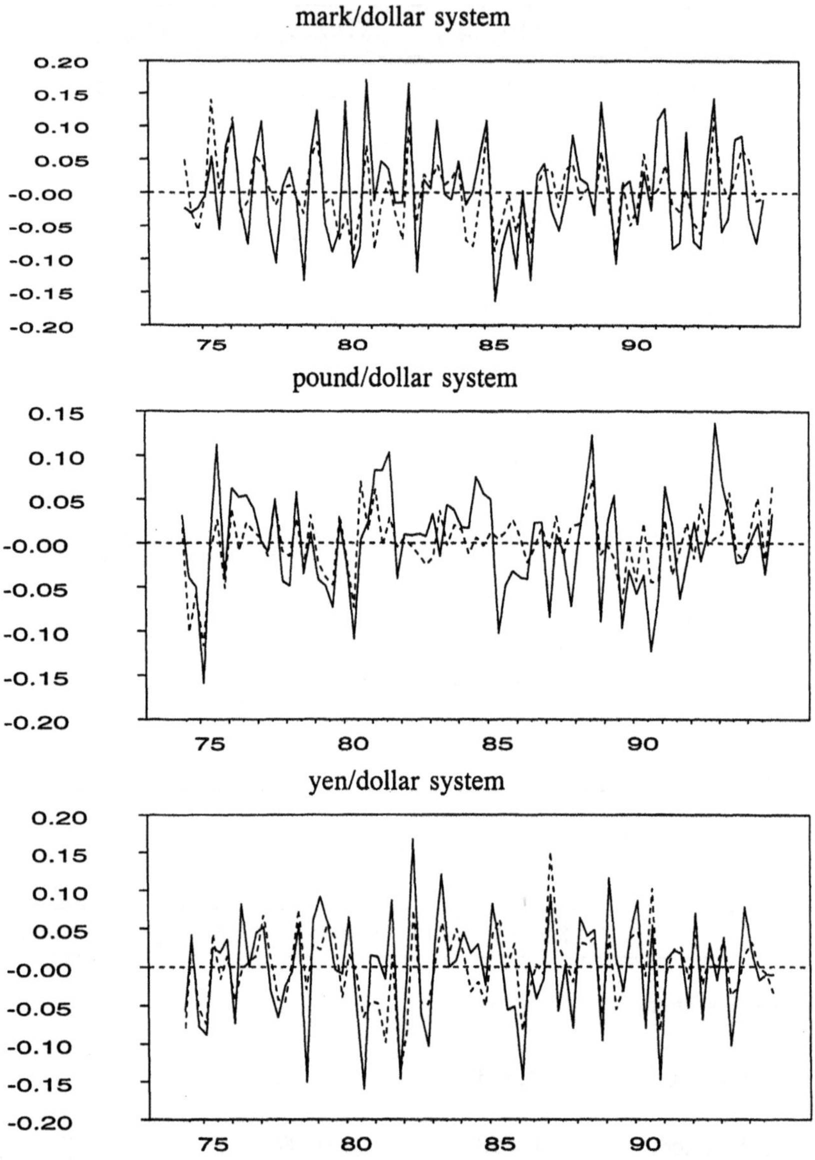

Figure 9: The estimated changes in the transitory components from the factor model (solid line) and from the SUR estimation (dashed line) with "News" as independent variables

(1977) was computed. It measures the adjustment fit for all three equations together and lies between 0 and 1. It is defined as follows[10]:

(4) $$R_*^2 = 1 - \frac{M}{tr(\hat{\Sigma}^{-1}S_{yy})}.$$

M is the number of equations in the SUR system. Here M is equal to 3. tr means "trace". $\hat{\Sigma}$ is the estimated variance covariance matrix of the residuals of each equation from the estimated SUR system. S_{yy} is the estimated variance covariance matrix of the dependent variables. The dependent variables are the first differences of the transitory components of the three real exchange rates. The value of this coefficient of determination in table 32 shows that the innovations are not able to explain a large part of the dependent variables.

In summary, the innovations cannot account for a large part of the changes in the transitory components of the three real exchange rates. In addition, many innovations have the wrong sign.

The procedure for constructing the innovations of the fundamentals might be criticized for several reasons. The innovations of one fundamental were constructed from the observations of the whole sample. Actually, they should have been constructed from the one-step ahead forecast errors of out-of-sample-forecasts. The author could not follow this procedure since he did not have enough observations to construct innovations from autoregressions for the seventies. A further problem might be that financial market participants do not form their rational expectations by autoregressions. However, market surveys show that many market participants perform chart analyses in the short run[11]. These market participants might use autoregressions to form their exchange rate expectations. Even if the results for the "news" approach are considered problematic, they coincide with the results of many other empirical studies which investigated the "news" approach and which did not construct the innovations from autoregressions. Examples are the empirical studies by Hardouvelis (1988) and Hakkio/Pearce (1985). They used survey data to determine expected changes of fundamentals. Not many innovations did have significant coefficients in their estimated equations although they used a much

---

[10]See Greene (1993, p. 491) for this definition.

[11]See Frankel/Froot (1987); Frankel/Froot, 1990, p. 95–102; Frankel/Froot, 1993b, p. 298–299; Frankel/Froot, 1993c, p. 324.

higher number of economics "news" variables. In summary, it seems that the "news" approach has not been very successful in explaining foreign exchange rate fluctuations. Thus it is correct to say that the transitory components of the three real exchange rates should not be well explained by innovations of the considered fundamentals.

These results imply that the three transitory components consist mainly of stationary excessive real exchange rate fluctuations. As was mentioned in section D. above, some types of excessive real exchange rate fluctuations from the transitory components can be excluded because they are nonstationary. But it is not possible to claim that the remaining causes of excessive exchange rate movements are responsible for the changes of the transitory components. The remaining explanations of excessive real exchange rate movements are just thinkable possibilities. This is, for example, true for the peso problems. Since the stochastic processes of the fundamentals were not tested for structural changes, exchange rate movements caused by peso problems do not have to be in the transitory components.

For reasons of positive economics it might be interesting to compute the duration of a shock with respect to the transitory components.

To determine the duration of a shock with respect to a transitory component, the impulse-response function was computed for every transitory component. To compute the impulse-response functions, every transitory component was identified with an autoregressive process of order k. The autoregressive process was then inverted to get the MA representation of that process and thus the response-impulse function.

For the transitory components of the mark/dollar, pound/dollar, and yen/dollar real exchange rate, the lag lengths for the autoregressive processes were chosen to be 5, 2, and 1 by using the BIC. Table 34 presents the Q statistics for the AR(k) models of the three different transitory components. The numbers in parantheses are degrees of freedom. The Q statistics were computed for 15 and 22 autocorrelations. The results in table table 34 show that the residuals of all three autoregressive processes are white noise at usual significance levels.

Sporadically, one or the other autocorrelation came relatively close to the boundaries of the interval $\pm 2.0/\sqrt{T}$[12]. Only the 22. autocorrelation of the autoregressive process for the transitory component of the mark/dollar real

[12]T means sample size here again.

	$Tq_{DM/\$}$	$Tq_{Pfund/\$}$	$Tq_{Yen/\$}$
Q(15)	12.234(10)	14.020(13)	17.246(14)
Q(22)	23.066(17)	17.887(20)	22.462(21)
MA constant	0.410	-12.004	6.291
Median lag	2–3	3–4	1–2
Mean lag	2.381	5.549	1.632

Table 34: The Q statistics for the residuals, the values of the constants in the MA models and the median und mean lag of the estimated stochastic processes of the transitory components of the three real exchange rates

exchange rate fell below the lower bound. This autocorrelation was interpreted as spurious.

Figure 10 shows the graphs of the MA coefficients (impulse-response functions) from the estimated MA processes of the transitory components for several lags. The graph for the mark/dollar real exchange rate shows that the effect of a shock fell below 0.1 after 8 to 9 quarters. Thus the constant of the MA process of the transitory component for the mark/dollar real exchange rate was almost realized after 8 to 9 quarters. For the pound/dollar and yen/dollar real exchange rate this period is 17 to 18 and 4 to 5 quarters, respectively. These values are similar to those of Huizinga (1987) although the real exchange rates reverted to their permanent components in his paper directly. The constants of the MA processes are given in the third row of table 34. This table also contains the values of the median and mean lag.

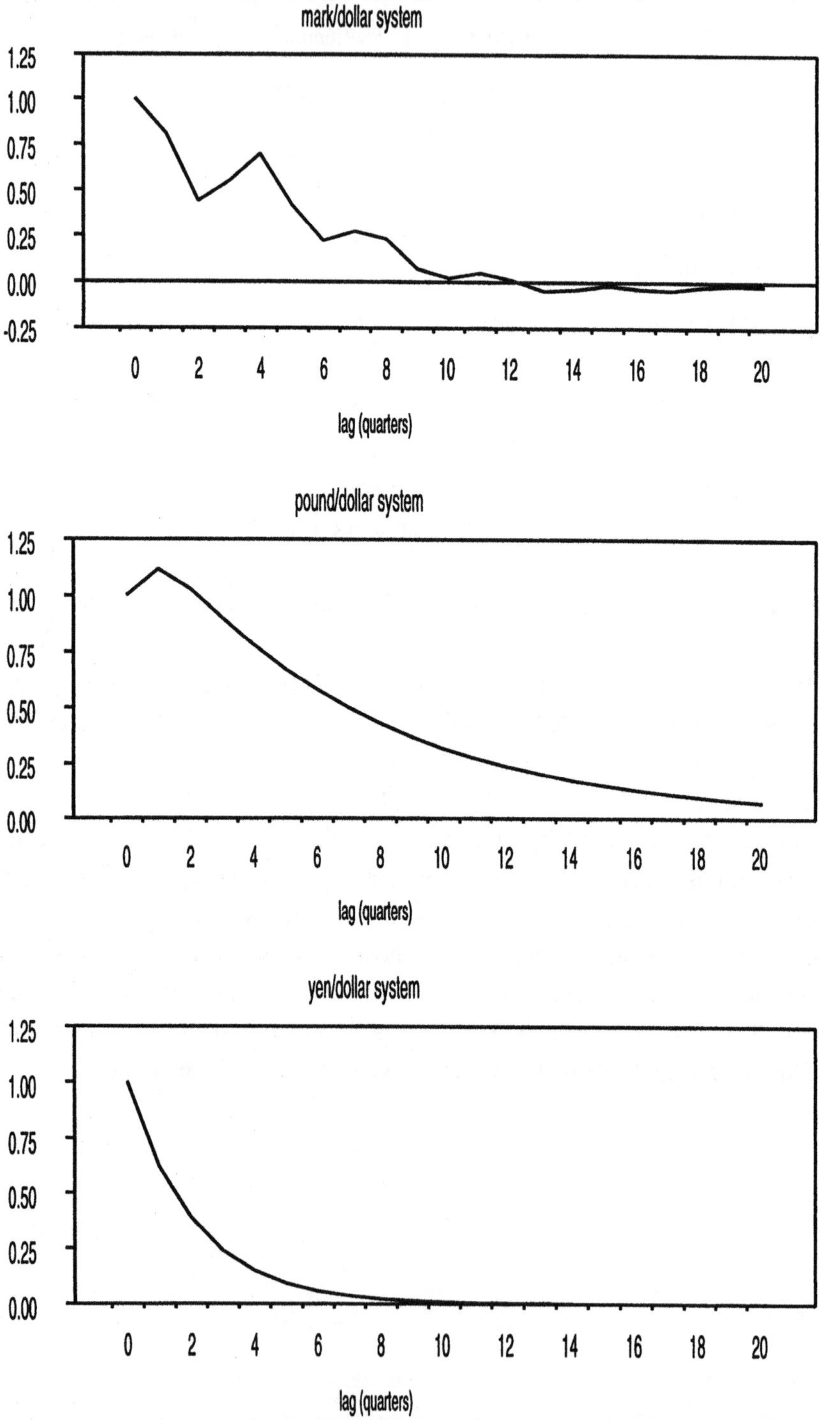

Figure 10: The impulse response functions of the estimated stochastic processes of the transitory components for the three real exchange rates

G. Results

One aim of this work was to explain the causes of the fluctuations in the mark/dollar, pound/dollar, and yen/dollar real exchange rate and to draw some policy conclusions from them. For every ECM, the fundamentals of the two-country overshooting model had at least some transitory influence on the corresponding real exchange rates. Changes in some fundamentals led also to changes of real exchange rates in the long-run. Moreover, the overshooting model also seems to have some power to explain movements of the three real exchange rates because the forecasting performance of the overshooting model in error correction form was satisfactory for the three exchange rate models. Since "news" with respect to fundamentals had little explanatory power to explain the movements of the considered real exchange rates, a large part of the transitory components had been due to causes of covariance-stationary excessive real exchange rate movements. Because of the stationarity of the transitory component nonstationary excessive real exchange movements can be excluded from the transitory components. These are real exchange rate movements caused by announced changes of stochastic processes of fundamentals (process switching or regime shifts), rational speculative bubbles, and learning processes. The weak evidence with respect to the last two causes of real exchange movements coincides with results of other empirical studies in the literature. Meese (1986), West (1987), and Frankel (1985) also tested for rational bubbles in some nominal exchange rates including the nominal counterparts of the real exchange rates considered in this paper. Mainly, they could not find evidence for rational speculative bubbles. Lewis (1989b) explored whether learning processes about the change in the US money demand function at the beginning of 1981 caused any part of the dollar appreciation in the first half of the eighties. She argues that market participants were uncertain about whether this change took place or not. They had to observe money demand data to learn the change of the US money demand function. By using conservative parameter values, learning processes were not able to explain much of the forecast errors in the first half of the eighties. Furthermore, the empirical evidence for peso problems is also weak. Kaminsky/Peruga (1991) and Krugman (1989a, p. 90) tried to explain the dollar appreciation in first half of the eigthies with peso problems. Kaminsky and Peruga argued that the market participants could have anticipated fiscal policy measures, that is, changes in the stochastic processes of fiscal variables, to depreciate the dollar. Kaminsky and Peruga (1991) used Lucas' (1982) asset pricing model to investigate this claim. They conclude that the expectation of a restrictive fiscal policy can not explain much of the dollar appreciation in the first half of the eighties. Krugman (1989a, p. 90) computes the probability under the peso problem hypothesis that the dollar had appreciated for five years in the first half of the eighties. This probability is just 0.068. Since this event has such a low probablity, peso problems could not have caused the dollar appreciation in the first half of the eighties according to Krugman. Krugman also argues that peso problems can not explain the dollar depreciation in the second half of the eighties either. In case of peso problems, the market would have had to expect a dollar appreciation for the second half of the eighties. But this expectation would have been unrealistic because of the high US trade deficits during this period. Presumably, a large part of the excessive exchange rate movements are due to irrational exchange rate expectations. At least survey data from financial markets show that exchange rate movements are determined by chartists in the short-run[1]. Krugman (1985, 1987, 1989b, p. 66–67) also gives empirical evidence for irrational exchange rate expectations for the three considered real exchange rates between 1985 and 1989. According to Krugman, financial market participants' expected dollar real depreciation was too low during this period. It was not compatible with high future US current account deficits and high US foreign indebtedness which would have had exploded under these foreign exchange rate expectations. However, financial market participants did not recognize the relationship among the dollar real exchange rate, the US current account, and the US foreign indebtedness because they were myopic. Thus the dollar stayed higher than it should have been.

A further question in this paper was which proposals for international monetary reform should be accepted for the three considered real exchange rates. Because the transitory components of the three real exchange rates are mainly determined by causes of real excessive exchange rate movements and because they are of some seize, the three real exchange rate systems should be reformed. That is, one of the policy recommendations of the second main group should be accepted.

Unfortunately, the proposals for reform of an exchange rate system to reduce excessive exchange rate movements have some problems as will be seen in the following. The systems of limited exchange rate flexibility (a fixed exchange rate regime with wide or narrow bands) to reduce excessive ex-

[1]See the quoted references in section F.

change rate movements are problematic for allocative reasons, as was pointed out in chapter A. since real shocks had permanent effects on real exchange rates[2]. However, this argument only holds if the quantitative effects of changes of the relevant fundamentals are sufficiently large. A similiar argument holds for foreign-exchange interventions. To see this, assume a positive permanent shock with respect to government expenditure. In the framework of Dornbusch's overshooting model with flexible exchange rates and perfect foresight, this fiscal shock leads to a nominal and real appreciation of the home currency without changes of the domestic price level. To keep the nominal exchange rate constant, the domestic central bank has to buy foreign exchange. If the foreign-exchange intervention is unsterilized[3], domestic money supply increases and the nominal exchange rate stays constant in the short-run. Because of the assumption of sluggish prices in Dornbusch's model, prices will start rising slowly. In the long-run, the real exchange rates will return to its level after the occurence of the fiscal shock because absolute purchasing power parity holds in Dornbusch's model in the long-run[4]. Although the nominal rate varies less in the long-run compared with the case without intervention nominal exchange rate variability has been replaced by more price variability. Even if absolute purchasing power parity does not hold, the higher domestic money supply should lead to higher prices in the long-run. Similar arguments can be made for real income shocks. Thus the objections raised against a system of limited nominal exchange rate flexibility can also be applied to foreign-exchange interventions since they lead to a higher price level variability when real shocks have permanent effects on real exchange rates. Again foreign exchange interventions are also again problematic for the other allocative reasons mentioned in section A. In addition, it is not clear whether foreign-exchange interventions are able to break market trends. For example, the German and Japanese central banks tried to stop the appreciation of their currencies by foreign-exchange interventions against the trend in spring 1986 and at the end of 1987. Despite their interventions the mark and the yen appreciated further. At least, it seems possible that central banks can reinforce a given trend in a foreign exchange market.

---

[2]Of course, the arguments in section A. also hold when only transitory changes in real variables lead to permanent changes in real exchange rates in the long-run.

[3]The Jurgensen Report (1983) suggested that only unsterilized foreign-exchange interventions have effects on nominal exchange rates.

[4]Branson (1986) already pointed out this problem of foreign-exchange interventions.

Moreover, it was shown in the literature that excessive real exchange rate movements (speculative attacks) can also appear in systems of limited exchange rate flexibility. Krugman (1979) and Obstfeld (1984, 1986) demonstrated this point for a system of fixed exchange rates under the assumption of rational expectations. Krugman and Rotemberg (1992) illustrated that speculative attacks can arise in systems of target zones if there is a stock of critical reserves and if market participants have rational expectations. Thus systems of limited exchange rate flexibility can not be used from the outset to reduce excessive real exchange rate movements.

Dornbusch and Frankel (1987, p. 49) pointed out that a dual exchange rate system also has problems in a full employment economy when permanent real shocks are present. An expansive fiscal policy can not lead to a real appreciation of the home currency and correspondingly to a worsening of the trade balance when the exchange rate for commercial transactions is fixed. If the trade balance can not deteriorate, the crowding out has to occur through a reduction of investment. Thus nominal and real interest rates have to rise and the reduction of investment will have adverse effects on growth. This argument is similar to Feldstein's in section A. In addition, the dual exchange rate system causes administrative and control costs. The latter criticism also holds for the Tobin tax. Finally, the Tobin tax would have to be implemented world-wide to avoid competitive distortions among financial places. Presumably, not every country would be willing to levy such a tax. In summary, in view of the problems of the proposals of the second main group, it is hard to choose one among these proposals. It is necessary to develop better proposals to reduce real excessive exchange rate movements.

Section A. dealt briefly with the intertemporal exchange rate theory under the assumption of flexible prices. According to this theory, real exchange rates should follow random walks. The test results in section C. showed that the random walk hypothesis could be rejected for the mark/dollar and pound/dollar real exchange rate. It was not clear whether the yen/dollar real exchange rate is a random walk or not because a lagged difference was added to the regression equation for the model with time trend. This was not done for the model which contained just a constant. The lagged difference implies a transitory component for the yen/dollar real exchange rate according to the Beveridge-Nelson decomposition. In summary, the evidence for the intertemporal theory under the assumption of flexible prices seems rather weak. The results from the tests with trivial cointegrating vectors and the factor model should not be used for judging the intertemporal foreign exchange theory under the assumption of flexible prices since these results were derived from a Keynesian model.

The results of this paper can also give some hints for stabilization policy. Monetary policy had some permanent or/and transitory effects influence on all three real exchange rates. Fiscal policy also influenced all three real exchange rates permanently or/and transitory through changes in government expenditure. Central banks and governments should take the employment effects of the real exchange rate changes into consideration when they decide on their policy measures. Furthermore, governments and central banks should also take the international repercussions of their measures through changes in foreign trade balances which are caused by real exchange rate changes into account. Finally, the results show that real income shocks also changed real exchange rates and therefore trade balances. Early advocates of flexible exchange rates claimed that every country could follow up its own employment and inflation targets. This claim has to be rejected because of the above mentioned results. The paper pleads for an international policy coordination to avoid beggar my neighbour policies and to neutralize the effects of income shocks. However, it is questionable whether such a policy coordination is feasible for political reasons.

There are also other empirical studies who found causal relationships between fiscal policy and real exchange rates including the real exchange rates which were considered in this paper. These studies used other models and estimation procedures to measure the influence of fiscal policy on real exchange rates. Some of these studies model fiscal policy with government expenditure[5] or with expected nominal or real, cyclical or structural budget deficits[6]. As was already mentioned, Kaminsky (1988) uses domestic (US) and foreign stocks of government bonds besides budget deficit-income ratios to model fiscal policy. Campbell and Clarida (1987) found significant effects of unexpected changes of equilibrium real exchange rates on real exchange rates by using a Kalman filter. Since unexpected changes of equilibrium real exchange rates are related to unexpected permanent real shocks their study also shows that real shocks had possessed some influence on real exchange rates. All these studies confirm the impression that fiscal policy and other real variables should have had some effect on the three real exchange rates

---

[5]See the studies of Evans (1986), Beltratti/Grilli (1989), and Froot/Rogoff (1991).

[6]See the empirical studies of Feldstein (1986), Hutchison/Throop (1985), Bahmani-Oskooe/Payesteh (1993), and the simulation studies of Knight/Masson (1988, 1990).

considered in this paper and other real exchange rates during the period of flexible nominal foreign exchange rates since 1973.

A second aim of this paper was to investigate the extent of covariance-stationarity of the three real exchange rates with the factor model of Gonzalo and Granger (1995). The results of the factor model showed that the three real exchange rates have covariance-stationary and nonstationary components to some extent. The stationarity of the three real exchange rates was also tested for in some other ways. The ERS test classified the mark/dollar and pound/dollar real exchange rate as covariance-stationary around a constant and the yen/dollar real exchange rate as an I(1) process, probably with a transitory component and a time trend. Thus relative purchasing power parity holds for the mark/dollar and pound/dollar real exchange rate according to the unit root tests. The results of the tests for trivial cointegrating vectors showed that three real exchange rates are I(1) processes. Thus the results with the respect to the stationarity of the mark/dollar and pound/dollar real exchange rate are contradictory. The results from the tests for trivial cointegrating vectors and from the factor model have to be criticized insofar as these results are derived from a particular model. On the other hand, the results are based on multivariate methods. In this respect, they are superior to the univariate unit root tests. This argument is again only of limited validity with respect to the test for trivial cointegrating vectors because - as was already mentioned in section D. - no Monte Carlo evidence exists with respect to the finite sample properties of this test especially under the assumption of non-normality. Despite these limitations, the three real exchange rates should probably be modelled as integrated processes with some covariance-stationary components in future models for real exchange rates according to the results from the tests for trivial cointegrating vectors and the factor model.

Appendix 1: The Cointegration Analysis for the Case of Stochastic Cointegration

The error correction model for the case of stochastic cointegration[1]:

$$\Delta X_t = \mu_0 + \alpha(\beta, \beta_1)'(X_{t-1}, t) + \sum_{i=1}^{k-1} \Gamma_i \Delta X_{t-i} + \phi D_t + \epsilon_t.$$

The residuals for all three systems behaved similiarly to those for the case of deterministic cointegration.

$H^*(r)$	trace statistic	λ_{max}	λ_i
$r = 0$	176.001[d]	62.828[d]	0.518
$r \leq 1$	113.173[a]	35.475	0.338
$r \leq 2$	77.698	26.234	0.263
$r \leq 3$	51.464	24.719	0.250
$r \leq 4$	26.745	13.128	0.142
$r \leq 5$	13.617	9.948	0.109
$r \leq 6$	3.669	3.669	0.042

Table 35: The values of the trace and maximal eigenvalue statistic for the mark/dollar system in the case of stochastic cointegration

[1]See Johansen (1994a, p. 212).

$H^*(r)$	trace statistic	λ_{max}	λ_i
r = 0	184.682[d]	56.894[d]	0.476
r ≤ 1	127.788[d]	43.606[a]	0.391
r ≤ 2	84.182[a]	33.944	0.320
r ≤ 3	50.238	24.343	0.242
r ≤ 4	25.895	13.048	0.138
r ≤ 5	12.847	8.311	0.090
r ≤ 6	4.536	4.536	0.050

Table 36: The values of the trace and maximal eigenvalue statistic for the pound/dollar system in the case of stochastic cointegration

$H^*(r)$	trace statistic	λ_{max}	λ_i
r = 0	187.310[d]	67.687[d]	0.537
r ≤ 1	119.623[c]	41.536[a]	0.376
r ≤ 2	78.087	34.273	0.323
r ≤ 3	43.814	18.961	0.194
r ≤ 4	24.853	11.692	0.124
r ≤ 5	13.161	9.044	0.098
r ≤ 6	4.116	4.116	0.046

Table 37: The values of the trace and maximal eigenvalue statistic for the yen/dollar system and the case of stochastic cointegration

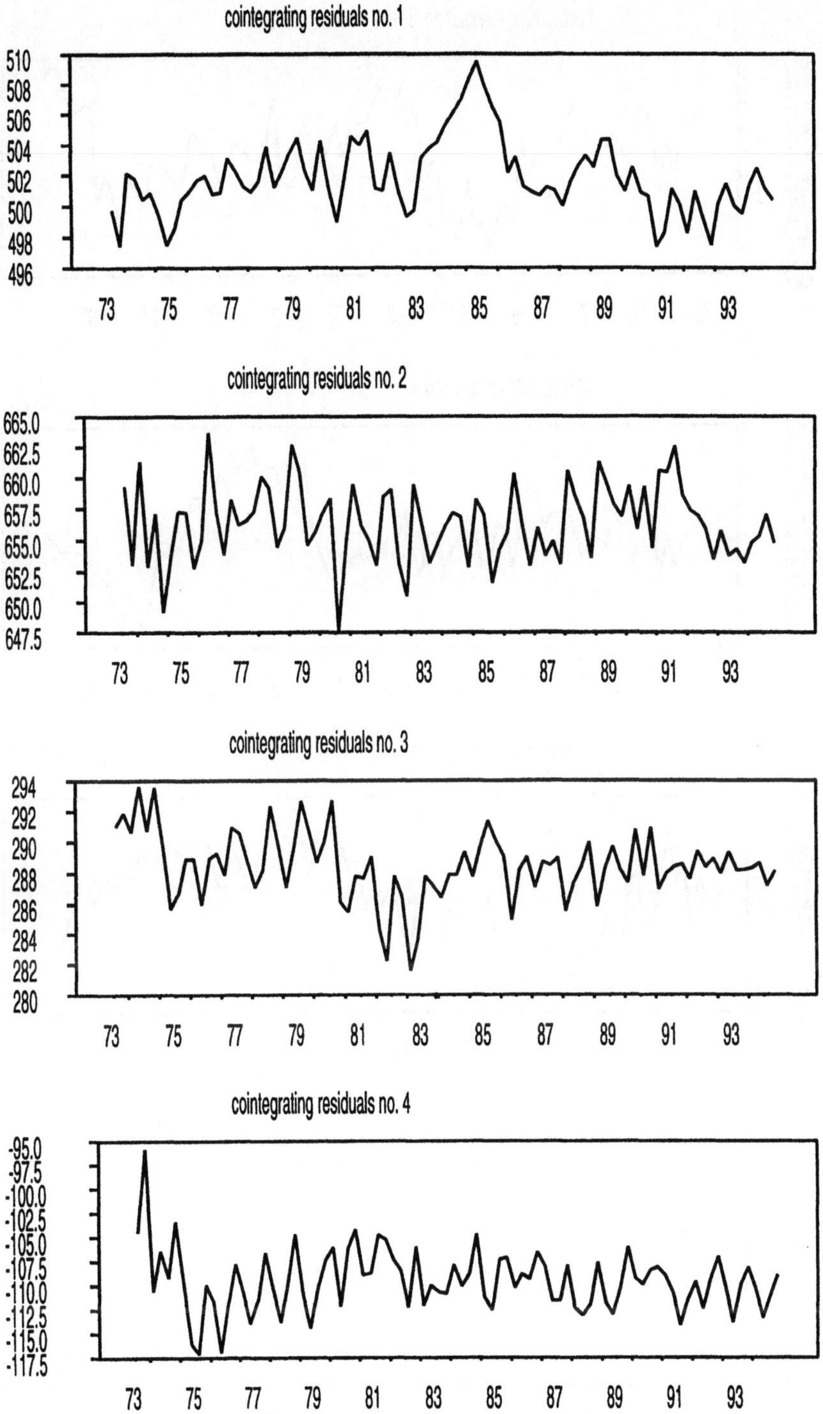

Figure 11: The cointegrating residuals for the mark/dollar system in the case of stochastic cointegration

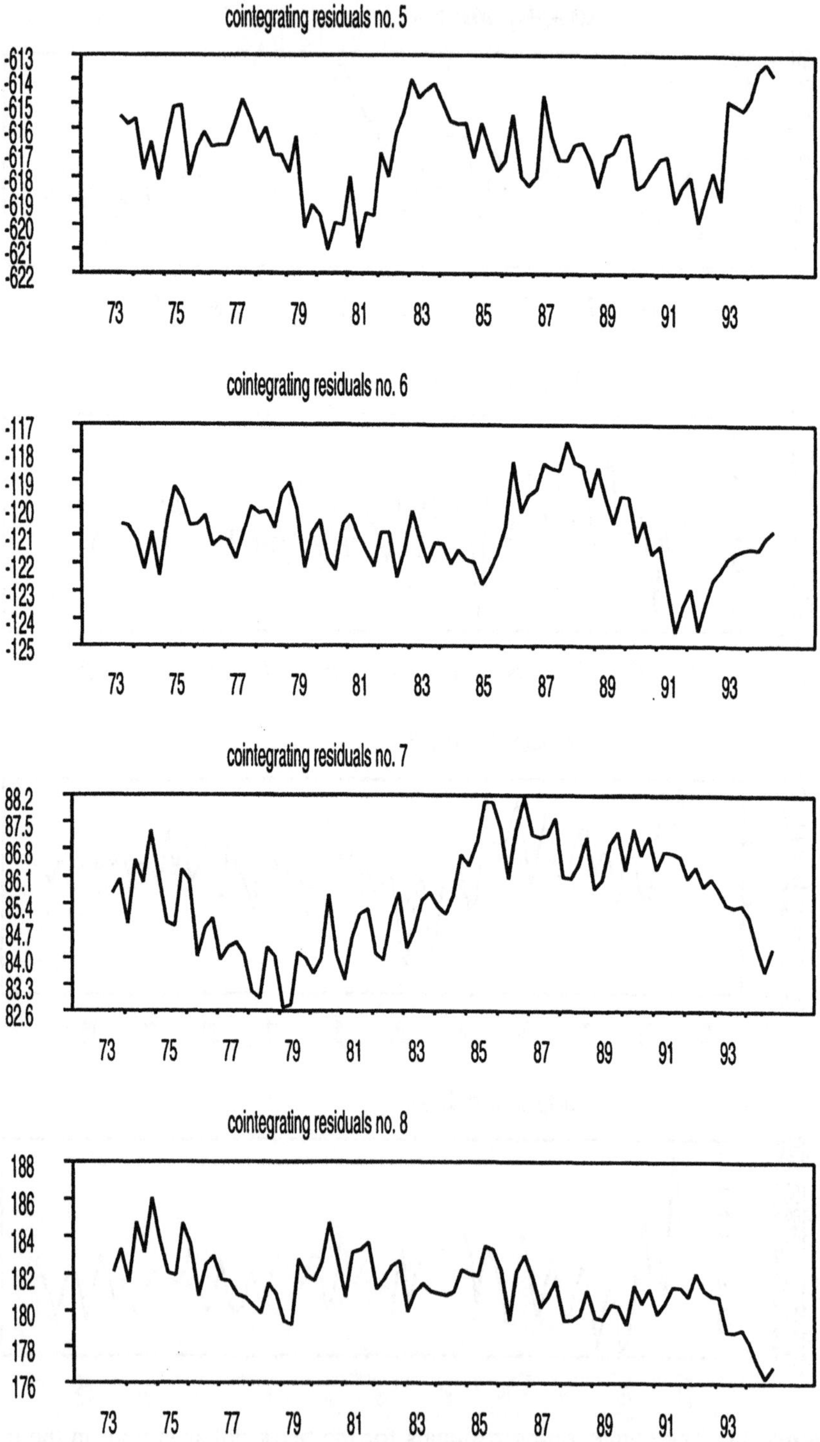

Continuation of figure 11

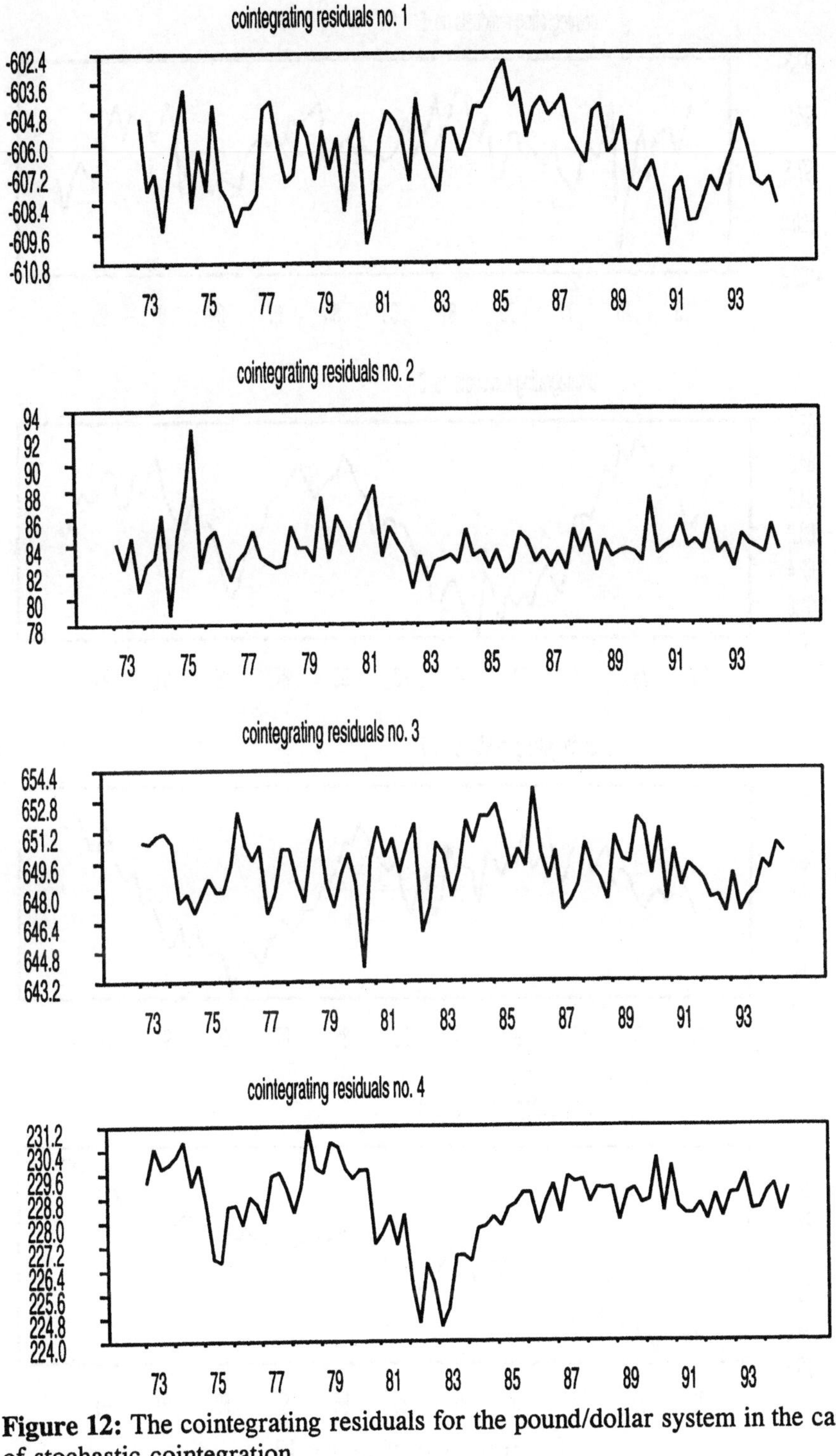

Figure 12: The cointegrating residuals for the pound/dollar system in the case of stochastic cointegration

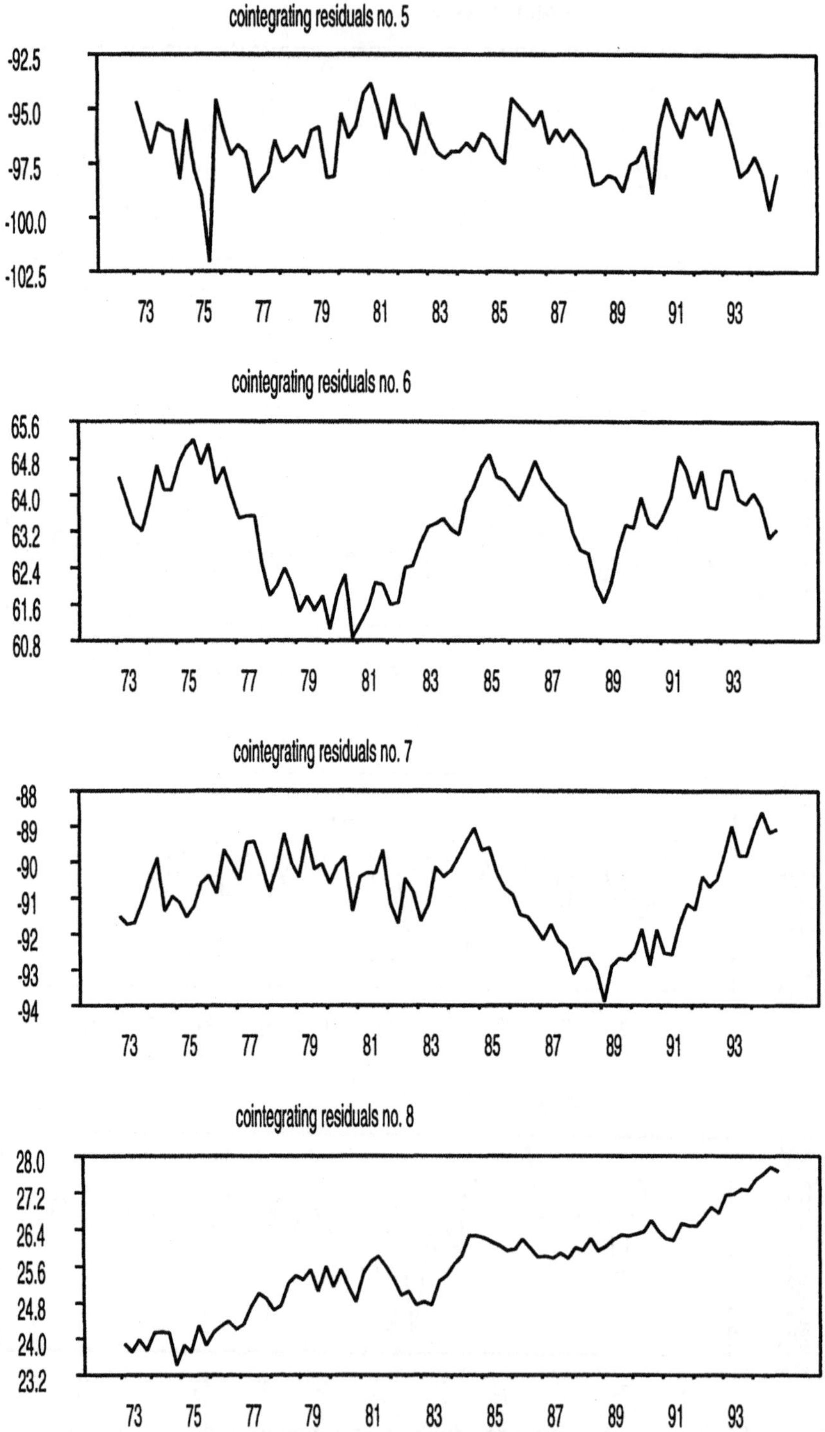

Continuation of figure 12

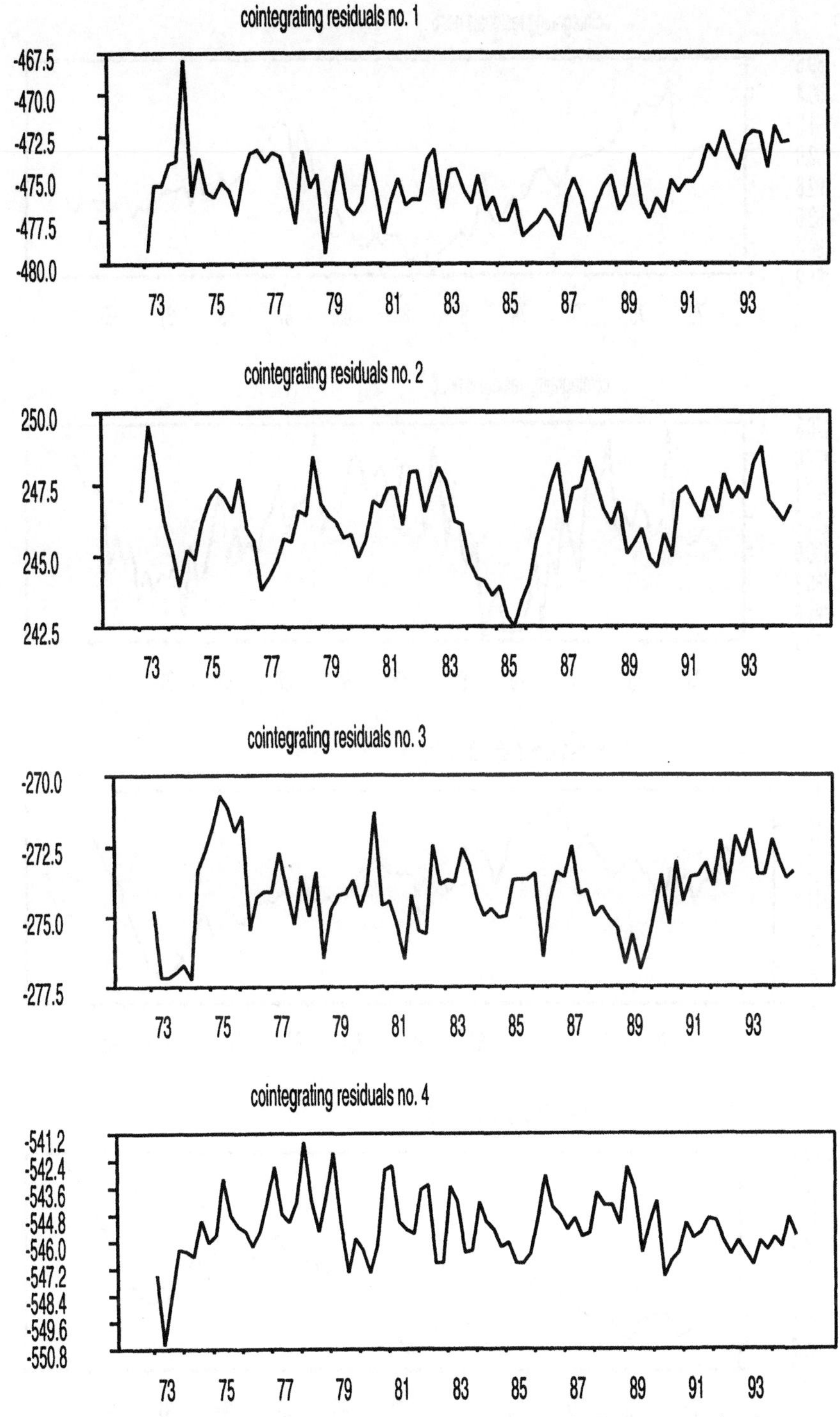

Figure 13: The cointegrating residuals for the yen/dollar system in the case of stochastic cointegration

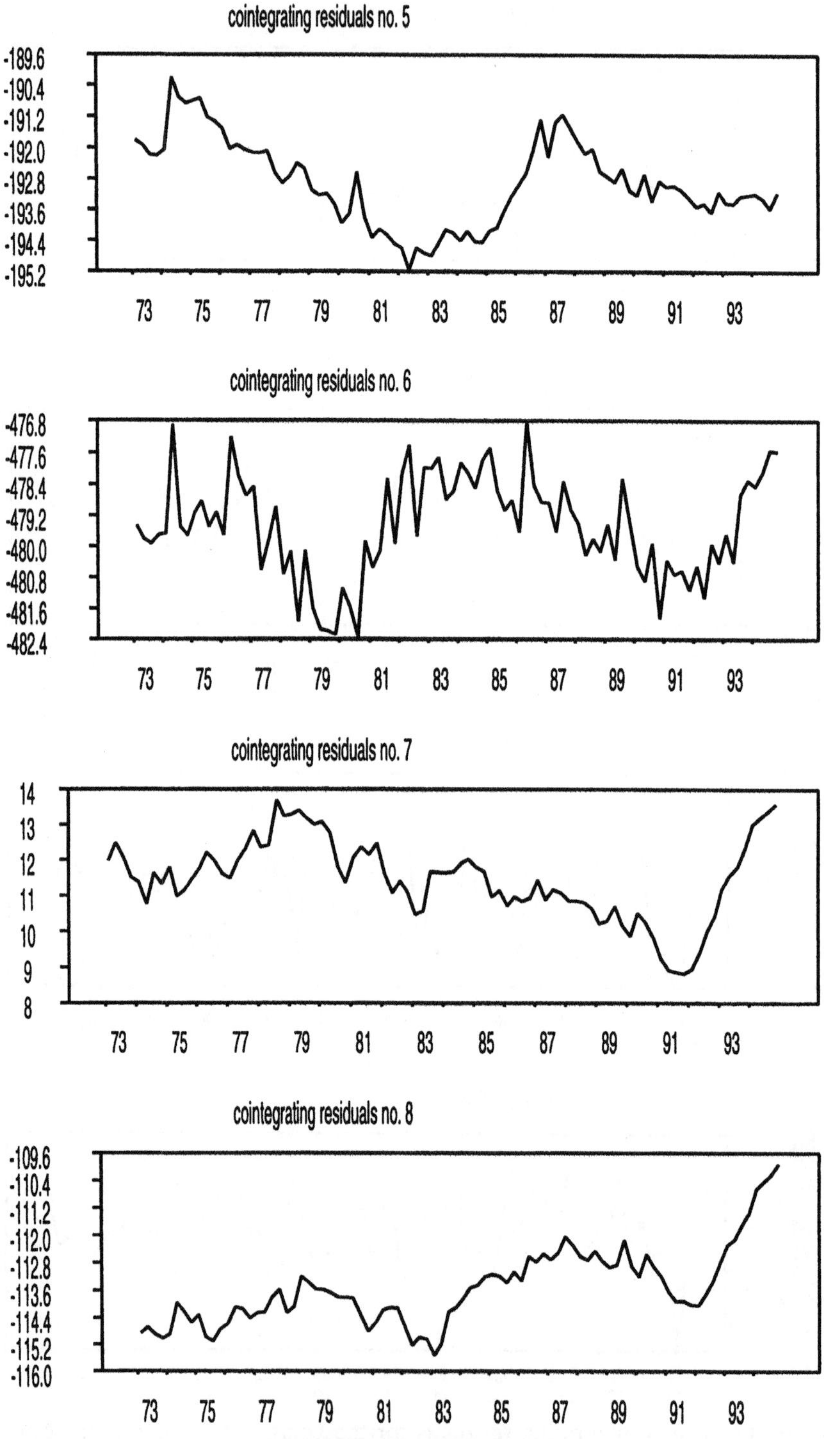

Continuation of figure 13

The chosen number of cointegrating vectors:
- mark/dollar system, $r \leq 4$
- pound/dollar system, $r \leq 3$
- yen/dollar system, $r \leq 4$

	mark/\$ system	pound/\$ system	yen/\$ system
LR statistic ~ $\chi^2(r)$	21.448[d]	8.729[b]	28.333[d]
r	$r \leq 4$	$r \leq 3$	$r \leq 4$

Table 38: The results of the tests for stochastic versus deterministic cointegration

variable	mark/\$ system	pound/\$ system	yen/\$ system
q_t	35.315[d]	24.225[d]	18.166[d]
$\bar{y}_t$	8.319[a]	28.031[d]	11.353[c]
$\bar{y}_t^*$	25.709[d]	16.507[d]	41.723[d]
$u_t - \bar{y}_t$	10.732[b]	24.031[d]	23.670[d]
$u_t^* - \bar{y}_t^*$	18.891[d]	18.475[a]	29.984[d]
r_t	16.043[d]	21.235[d]	38.262[d]
r_t^*	20.042[d]	11.987[d]	19.275[d]
$r[(p + 1) - s]$	4	3	4

Table 39: The results of the tests for exclusion of a parameter of one variable from all cointegrating vectors in the case of stochastic cointegration

eq.	mark/$ system	pound/$ system	yen/$ system
1. eq.	16.877[d]	2.813	18.807[d]
2. eq.	6.838	18.425[d]	13.245[c]
3. eq.	8.60[a]	1.556[d]	17.746[d]
4. eq.	5.550	5.449	10.550[b]
5. eq.	26.023[d]	10.942[c]	28.291[d]
6. eq.	8.808[a]	17.956[d]	21.544[d]
7. eq.	12.524[c]	10.334[c]	6.368
r(p - m)	4	3	4

Table 40: The results of the tests for weak exogeneity of a single variable in the case of stochastic cointegration

	mark/$ system	pound/$ system	yen/$ system
LR statistic ~ $\chi^2[(p - r)r_1]$	14.437[d]	21.316[d]	16.364[d]
$(p - r)r_1$	3	4	3

Table 41: The results of the tests for trivial cointegrating vectors with respect to the three real exchange rates in the case of stochastic cointegration

variable	mark/$ system	pound/$ system	yen/$ system
q_{t-1}	-0.328[a]	-0.097[b]	-0.308[d]
$\bar{y}_{t-1}$	-0.980[a]	0.308	0.549[c]
$\bar{y}^*_{t-1}$	-1.145[a]	0.079	-1.047[c]
$u_{t-1} - \bar{y}_{t-1}$	-0.327[d]	0.383	0.060
$u^*_{t-1} - \bar{y}^*_{t-1}$	0.079	0.009	-0.043
r_{t-1}	0.035	-0.008	-0.023[c]
r^*_{t-1}	0.023	0.013	0.042[d]

Table 42: The results for the tests of significance of the parameters in $\Pi = [\alpha, (\beta, \beta_1)]$ for the equation of the real exchange rate in all three ECMs (stochastic cointegration)

Table 43: The results for the tests of significance of the parameters in Γ_i, i = 1, ..., k - 1, and Φ for the equation of the real exchange rate in all three ECMs (stochastic cointegration)

variable	mark/$ system	pound/$ system	yen/$ system
Δq_{t-1}	0.393[a]	0.343[d]	0.325[a]
Δq_{t-2}	0.053	-0.199[a]	0.097
Δq_{t-3}	0.271[a]		
Δq_{t-4}	0.145		
$\Delta \bar{y}_{t-1}$	-0.504	-0.438	-0.461
$\Delta \bar{y}_{t-2}$	1.106	0.708	1.096
$\Delta \bar{y}_{t-3}$	2.593[a]		
$\Delta \bar{y}_{t-4}$	0.592		
$\Delta \bar{y}^*_{t-1}$	4.233[a]	0.773	1.342
$\Delta \bar{y}^*_{t-2}$	-0.105	-0.364	0.424

variable	mark/$ system	pound/$ system	yen/$ system
$\Delta\bar{y}^*_{t-3}$	-0.774		
$\Delta\bar{y}^*_{t-4}$	1.405		
$\Delta(u_{t-1} - \bar{y}_{t-1})$	-0.221	-0.604	-0.003
$\Delta(u_{t-2} - \bar{y}_{t-2})$	1.052[c]	0.379	-0.450
$\Delta(u_{t-3} - \bar{y}_{t-3})$	1.529[a]		
$\Delta(u_{t-4} - \bar{y}_{t-4})$	0.127		
$\Delta(u^*_{t-1} - \bar{y}^*_{t-1})$	2.990[a]	1.551[a]	2.005[a]
$\Delta(u^*_{t-2} - \bar{y}^*_{t-2})$	-0.140	-1.297[a]	-0.405
$\Delta(u^*_{t-3} - \bar{y}^*_{t-3})$	-0.859		
$\Delta(u^*_{t-4} - \bar{y}^*_{t-4})$	-0.316		
Δr_{t-1}	-0.011	0.001	0.026[a]
Δr_{t-2}	-0.004	0.000	0.026[a]
Δr_{t-3}	-0.008		
Δr_{t-4}	0.017		
Δr^*_{t-1}	0.004	0.011	-0.012
Δr^*_{t-2}	0.027	0.009	-0.006
Δr^*_{t-3}	0.031[c]		
Δr^*_{t-4}	-0.013		
D_{1t}	0.000	-0.001	-0.017
D_{2t}	0.008	-0.008	0.009
D_{3t}	0.000	0.006	0.024

Continuation of table 43

Appendix 2: The Description of the Data and Their Sources

The nominal exchange rates, consumer price indices, and nominal interest rates are from the "Rheinisch-Westfälisches Institut für Wirtschaftsforschung" in Essen (Germany). The German gross domestic product and government expenditure (government consumption and investment) were obtained from the Federal Statistical Office in Wiesbaden (Germany). The numbers with respect to the US gross domestic product and US government expenditure were made available to the author by the "Institut der deutschen Wirtschaft" in Cologne (Germany). The output and government expenditure series of the other countries (United Kingdom and Japan) stem from the data bank of the company DATASTREAM INTERNATIONAL, London. The time series from this data bank are listed under the section "National Government Series" in the code book of this company.

All data refer to the sample period first quarter 1972 to the fourth quarter 1994.

Germany:

Consumer price indices. Source: IMF, International Financial Statistics, row 64. Frequency: monthly, seasonally unadjusted.

Nominal exchange rates (mark/dollar). Source: IMF, International Financial Statistics, row rf. Frequency: monthly. Monthly averages.

3-month interbank deposit rate. Source: IMF, International Financial Statistics, row 60bs. Frequency: monthly.

Gross domestic product in billions of marks. Source: Federal Statistical Office. Frequency: quarterly. In constant prices, seasonally adjusted.

Government consumption in billions of marks. Source: Federal Statistical Office. Frequency: quarterly. In constant prices, seasonally adjusted.

Gross government building investment expenditure and gross government investment expenditure in plant and equipment in billions of marks. Source: Federal Statistical Office. Frequency: quarterly. In constant prices, seasonally adjusted.

United Kingdom:

Retail prices. Source: IMF, International Financial Statistics, row 64. Frequency: monthly. Seasonally unadjusted.

Nominal exchange rate (pound/dollar). Source: IMF, International Financial Statistics, row rf. Frequency: monthly. Monthly averages.

3-month treasury bill rate. Source: IMF, International Financial Statistics, row 60c. Frequency: monthly.

Gross domestic product to market prices in millions of pounds. Source: National Government Series. Frequency: quarterly. In constant prices, seasonally adjusted.

Government consumption expenditure in millions of pounds. Source: National Government Series. Frequency: quarterly. In constant prices, seasonally adjusted.

Government investment expenditure for fixed capital in millions of pounds. Source: National Government Series. Frequency: quarterly. In constant prices, seasonally adjusted.

Japan:

Consumer price indices. Source: IMF, International Financial Statistics, row 64. Frequency: monthly, seasonally unadjusted.

Nominal exchange rates (yen/dollar). Source: IMF, International Financial Statistics, row rf. Frequency: monthly. Monthly averages.

3-month money market rate. Source: IMF, International Financial Statistics, row 60b. Frequency: monthly.

Gross national product in billions of yen at annual rates: National Government Series. Frequency: quarterly. In constant prices, seasonally adjusted.

Goverment consumption expenditure in billions of yen at annual rates. Source: National Government Series. Frequency: quarterly. In constant prices, seasonally adjusted.

Government investment expenditure in fixed capital in billions of yen at annual rates. Source: National Government Series. Frequency: quarterly. In constant prices, seasonally adjusted.

USA:

Consumer price indices. Source: IMF, International Financial Statistics, row 64. Frequency: monthly. Seasonally unadjusted.

3-month treasury bill rate. Source: IMF, International Financial Statistics, row 60c. Frequency: monthly.

Gross domestic product in billions of dollars at annual rates. Source: OECD, Main Economic Indicators. Frequency: quarterly. In constant prices, seasonally adjusted.

Government consumption and investment (in fixed capital) expenditure in billlions of dollars at annual rates. Source: OECD, Main Economic Indicators. Frequency: quarterly. In constant prices, seasonally adjusted.

Abbreviations

AR	Autoregressive
ARCH	Autoregressive Conditional Heteroscedasticity
ARMA	Autoregressive Moving Average
BIC	Bayesian Information Criterion
C	constant
ECM	Error Correction Model
EMS	European Monetary System
eq.	equation
ERS	Elliott, Rothenberg, and Stock
GDP	Gross Domestic Product
GLS	Generalized Least Squares
GNP	Gross National Product
I(1)	integrated of order 1
I(0)	integrated of order 0
J.-B.	Jarque-Bera
LR	Likelihood Ratio
MA	Mean Error or Moving Average
MAE	Mean Absolute Error
ML	Maximum Likelihood
OLS	Ordinary Least Squares
P	permanent component
T	sample size or transitory component
tr	trace
tre	trend
RMSE	Root Mean Square Error
SUR	Seemingly Unrelated Regression
VAR	Vektorautoregressive System

List of Figures

List of Tables

References

Azariadis, C. (1993): "Intertemporal Macroeconomics". Cambridge, Massachusetts.

Bahmani-Oskooe, M./Payesteh, S. (1993): "Budget Deficits and the Value of the Dollar: An Application of Cointegration and Error-Correction Modeling", in: Journal of Macroeconomics, Vol. 15, No. 4, p. 661–77.

Beltratti, A./Grilli, V. (1989): "U.S. Military Expenditure and the Dollar", in: Economic Inquiry, Vol. 27, p. 737–744.

Beveridge, S./Nelson, C.R. (1981): "A New Approach to Decomposition of Economic Time Series into Permanent and Transitory Components with Particular Attention to Measurement of the 'Business Cyle'", in: Journal of Monetary Econmics, Vol. 7, p. 151-174.

Blanchard, O.J./Fischer, S. (1989): "Lectures on Macroeconomics". Cambridge, Massachusettes.

Box, G.E.P./Pierce, D.A. (1970): "Distribution of Residual Autocorrelations in Autoregressive Integrated Moving Average Time Series Models, in: Journal of the American Statistical Association, Vol. 65, p. 1509–1526.

Box, G.E.P./Ljung, G.M. (1978): "On a Measure of Lack of Fit in Time Series Models", in: Biometrika, Vol. 65, p. 297–300.

Branson, W.H. (1985): "Causes of Appreciation and Volatility of the Dollar". NBER Working Paper No. 1777.

Branson, W. H. (1986): "The Limits of Monetary Coordination As Exchange Rate Policy", in: Brookings Papers of Economic Activity, Vol. 1, p. 175–192.

Buiter, W.H. (1988): "Macroeconomic Policy Design in an Interdependent World Economy: An Analysis of Three Contingencies", in: Frenkel, J.A. (ed.): "International Aspects of Fiscal Policies". Chicago, p. 121–155.

Campbell, J.Y./Clarida R.H. (1987): "The Dollar and Real Interest Rates", in: Carnegie-Rochester Conference Series on Public Policy, Vol. 27, p. 103–139.

Campbell, J.Y./Perron, P. (1993): "A Note on Johansen's Cointegration Procedure When Trends Are Present", in: Empirical Economics, Vol. 18, p. 777–789.

Cheung, Y.-W./Lai, K.S. (1993): "Finite-Sample Sizes of Johansen's Likelihood Ratio Tests for Cointegration", in: Oxford Bulletin of Economics and Statistics, Vol. 55, No. 3, p. 313-328.

Cheung, Y.-W./Lai, K.S. (1994): "Mean Reversion in Real Exchange Rates", in: Economics Letters, Vol. 46, p. 251-256.

Dickey, D.A./Fuller, W.A. (1979): "Distribution of the Estimators for Autoregressive Time Series with a Unit Root", in: Journal of the American Statistical Association, Vol. 74, No. 366, p. 427-431.

Dickey, D.A./Said, S.E. (1984): "Testing for Unit Roots in ARMA Models of Unknown Order", in: Biometrika, Vol. 71, p. 599-607.

Dornbusch, R. (1976): "Expectations and Exchange Rate Dynamics", in: Journal of Political Economy, Vol. 84, No. 6, p. 1161-1176.

Dornbusch, R. (1982): "Equilibrium and Disequilibrium Exchange Rates", in: Zeitschrift für Wirtschafts- und Sozialwissenschaften, Vol. 102, No. 6, p. 573-599.

Dornbusch, R./Frankel, J. (1987): "The Flexible Exchange Rate System: Experience and Alternatives". NBER Working Paper, No. 2464.

Edwards, S. (1982): "Exchange Rates and News: A Multi-Currency Approach", in: Journal of International Money and Finance, Vol. 1, p. 211-224.

Eichengreen, B./Wyplosz, C. (1993): "The Unstable EMS", in: Brookings Papers on Economic Activity, Vol. 1, p. 51-143.

Eitrheim, O. (1992): "Inference in Small Cointegrated Systems: Some Monte Carlo Results". Discussion paper, 92-31, Department of Economics, University of California, San Diego, La Jolla, USA.

Elliott, G./Rothenberg, T.J./Stock, J.H. (1992): "Efficient Tests for an Autoregressive Unit Root". NBER Technical Working Paper No. 130.

Engle, R.F./Granger, C.W.J. (1987): "Cointegration and Error Correction: Representation, Estimation, and Testing", in: Econometrica, Vol. 55, No. 2, p. 251-276.

Evans, P. (1986): "Is the Dollar High because of Large Budget Deficits ?", in: Journal of Monetary Econmics, Vol. 18, p. 227-249.

Feldstein, M. (1986): "The Budget Deficit and the Dollar", in: NBER Macroeconmics. Annual. Cambridge, Massachusettes, p. 355-392.

Feldstein, M. (1994): "American Economic Policy in the 1980s: A Personal View", in: Feldstein, M. (ed.): "American Economic Policy in the 1980s". National Bureau of Economic Research Conference Report. Chicago.

Flood R.P./Hodrick, R.J. (1986): "Asset Price Volatility, Bubbles and Process Switching", in: Journal of Finance, Vol. 41, No. 4, p. 831-842.

Frankel, J.A. (1982): "In Search of the Exchange Risk Premium: A Six-Currency Test Assuming Mean-Variance Optimization", in: Journal of International Monetary and Finance, Vol. 1, p. 255-274.

Frankel, J.A. (1985): "The Dazzling Dollar", in: Brookings Paper of Economic Activity, Vol. 1, p. 199-217.

Frankel, J.A./Froot, K.A. (1987): "Using Survey Data to Test Standard Propositions Regarding Exchange Rate Expectations", in: American Economic Review, Vol. 77, No. 1, p. 133-153.

Frankel, J.A./Froot, K.A. (1990): "Chartists, Fundamentalists and the Demand for Dollars", in: Courakis, A.S./Taylor, M.P. (eds.): "Private Behavior and Government Policy in Interdependent Economies". Oxford, p. 73-126

Frankel, J.A./Froot, K.A. (1993a): "Forward Discount Bias: "Is It an Exchange Risk Premium?", in: Frankel, J.A. (eds.): "On Exchange Rates". Cambridge, Massachusetts, p. 245-260.

Frankel, J.A./Froot, K.A. (1993b): "Understanding the U.S. Dollar in the Eighties: The Expectations of Chartists and Fundamentalists", in: Frankel (ed.): "On Exchange Rates". Cambridge, Massachusetts, p. 295-316.

Frankel, J.A./Froot, K.A. (1993c): "Chartists, Fundamentalists, and Trading in the Foreign Exchange Market", in: Frankel, J.A. (ed.): "On Exchange Rates". Cambridge, Massachusetts, p. 317-326.

Frenkel, J.A. (1981): "Flexible Exchange Rates, Prices, and the Role of 'News': Lessons from the 1970's", in: Journal of Political Economy, Vol. 89, No. 4, p. 665-705.

Frenkel, J. (1985): "Comment on 'Causes of Appreciation and Volatility of the Dollar'. NBER Working Paper No. 1777.

Frenkel, J.A. (1987): "The International Monetary System: Should it be Reformed?", in: American Economic Review, Vol. 77, No. 2, p. 205–210.

Frenkel J.A./Mussa, M.L. (1980): "The Efficiency of Foreign Exchange Markets and Measures of Turbulence", in: American Economic Review Papers and Proceedings, Vol. 70, No. 2, p. 374–381.

Friedman, M. (1953): "The Case for Flexible Exchange Rates", in: Friedman, M.: "Essays in Positive Economics". Chicago, p. 157–227.

Froot, K.A./Rogoff, K. (1991): "Government Spending and the Real Exchange Rate: The Empirical Evidence". Mimeo, presented at the NBER summer institute on August 16, 1991, USA.

Froot, K.A./Rogoff, K. (1994): Perspectives on PPP and Long-Run Real Exchange Rates", in: Grossman, G./Rogoff, K. (eds.): "Handbook of International Economics", Vol. 3. Amsterdam.

Gonzalo, J. (1994): "Five Alternative Methods of Estimating Long-Run Equilibrium Relationships", in: Journal of Econometrics, Vol. 60, p. 203–133.

Gonzalo, J./Granger, C.W.J. (1995): "Estimation of Common Long-Memory Components in Cointegrated Systems", in: Journal of Business & Economic Statistics, Vol. 13, No. 1, p. 27–35.

Granger, C.W.J./Newbold, P. (1986): "Forecasting Economic Time Series". Second edition. Orlando, Florida.

Greene, W.H. (1993): Econometric Analysis. Second edition. New York.

Hakkio, C.S./Pearce, D.K. (1985): "The Reaction of Exchange Rates to Economic News", in: Economic Inquiry, Vol, 23, No. 4, p. 621–636.

Hardouvelis, G.A. (1988): "Economic News, Exchange Rates, and Interest Rates", in: Journal of International Money and Finance, Vol. 7, No. 1, p. 23–35.

Hodrick, R.J./Srivastava, S. (1984): "An Investigation of Risk and Return in Forward Foreign Exchange", in: Journal of International Money and Finance, Vol. 3, p. 5–29.

Huizinga, J. (1987): "An Empirical Investigation of the Long-Run Behavior of Real Exchange Rates", in: Carnegie-Rochester Conference Series on Public Policy, Vol. 27, p. 149–214.

Hutchison, M./Throop, A. (1985): "U.S. Budget Deficits and the Real Value of the Dollar", in: Economic Review of the Federal Bank of San Francisco, Fall, p. 26-43.

Johansen, S./Juselius, K. (1990): "Maximum Likelihood Estimation and Inference on Cointegration - With Applications to the Demand for Money", in: Oxford Bulletin of Economics and Statistics, Vol. 52, No. 2, p. 169-210.

Johansen, S. (1991): "Estimation and Hypothesis Testing of Cointegration Vectors in Gaussian Vector Autoregressive Models", in: Econometrica, Vol. 59, No. 6, p. 1551-1580.

Johansen, S./Juselius, K. (1992): "Testing Structural Hypotheses in a Multivariate Cointegration Analysis of the PPP and the UIP for UK", in: Journal of Econometrics, Vol. 53, p. 211-244.

Johansen, S. (1992): "Determination of Cointegration Rank in the Presence of a Linear Trend", Oxford Bulletin of Economics and Statistics, Vol. 54, No. 3, p. 383-397.

Johansen, S. (1994a): "The Role of the Constant and Linear Terms in Cointegration Analysis of Nonstationary Variables", in: Econometric Reviews, Vol. 13, No. 2, p. 205-229.

Johansen, S. (1994b): "Estimating Systems of Trending Variables", in: Econometric Reviews, 1994, Vol. 13, No. 3, p. 351-386.

Johansen, S. (1995): "Likelihood-Based Inference on Cointegrated Vector Autoregressive Models". Oxford.

Johnson, H. (1972): "The Case for Flexible Exchange Rates, 1969", in: "Further Essays in Monetary Economics". Cambridge, Massachusetts, p. 198-222.

Jurgensen Report (1983): "Report of the Working Group on Exchange Market Intervention". U.S. Treasury.

Kaminsky, G. (1988): "The Real Exchange Rate since Floating: Market Fundamentals or Bubbles?". Mimeo, Department of Economics, University of California, San Diego, La Jolla, USA.

Kaminsky, G./Peruga, R. (1991): "Credibility Crises: The Dollar in the Early 1980s", in: Journal of International Money and Finance, Vol. 10, p. 170-192.

Knight, M./Masson, P.R. (1988): "Fiscal Policies, Net Saving, and Real Exchange Rates: The United States, the Federal Republic of Germany, and Japan", in: Frenkel, J.A. (ed.): "International Aspects of Fiscal Policies". Chicago, p. 21-61.

Kostial, K. (1994): "The Role of the Signal-Noise Ratio in Cointegrated Systems". Mimeo, presented at the conference of the Econometric Society in Maastricht. European University Institute, Economics Department, Florence, Italy.

Krugman, P.R. (1979): "A Model of Balance of Payments Crises", in: Journal of Money, Credit and Banking, Vol. 11, p. 311-325.

Krugman, P.R. (1985): "Is the Strong Dollar Sustainable?". NBER Working Paper No. 1644.

Krugman, P.R. (1987): "Sustainability and the Decline of the Dollar", in: Bryant, R./Holtham, G./Hooper, P. (eds.): "External Deficits and the Dollar". Washington, D.C, p. 82-99.

Krugman, P. R. (1989a): "Exchange Rate Instability". Cambridge, Massachusetts.

Krugman, P. R.(1989b): "The Case for Stabilizing Exchange Rates", in: Oxford Review of Economic Policy, Vol. 5, No. 3, p. 61-72.

Krugman, P.R./Rotemberg, J. (1992): "Speculative Attacks on Target Zones", in: Krugman, P./Miller, M. (eds.): "Exchange Rate Targets and Currency Bands". Cambridge, Massachusetts, p. 117-132.

Landmann, O. (1988): "Current Issues in the International Macroeconomic Policy Debate", in: Borner, S. (ed.): "International Finance and Trade in a Polycentric World". London, p. 307-321.

Levich, R.M. (1985): "Gauging the Evidence on Recent Movements in the Value of the Dollar", in: "The US Dollar Recent Developments - Outlook, and Policy Options". A Symposium Sponsored by The Federal Reserve Bank of Kansas City, p. 1-27.

Levich, R.M. (1989): "Is the Foreign Exchange Market Efficient?", in: Oxford Review of Economic Policy, Vol. 5, No. 3, p. 40-60.

Lewis, K.K. (1988a): "Inflation Risk and Asset Market Disturbances: The Mean Variance Model Revisited", in: Journal of International Money and Finance, Vol. 7, p. 273-288.

Lewis, K.K. (1988b): "The Persistence of the 'Peso Problem' When Policy is Noisy", in: Journal of International Money and Finance, Vol. 7, p. 1-21.

Lewis, K.K. (1989a): "Can Learning Affect Exchange-Rate Behavior? The Case of the Dollar in the Early 1980's", in: Journal of Monetary Economics, Vol. 23, p. 79-100.

Lewis, K.K. (1989b): "Changing Beliefs and Systematic Rational Forecast Errors with Evidence from Foreign Exchange", in: American Economic Review, Vol. 79, No. 4, p. 621-636.

Lewis, K.K. (1992): "Peso Problems", in: Newman, P./Milgate, M./Eatwell, J. (eds.): "New Palgrave Dictionary of Money and Finance", Vol. 2, p. 140-142.

Lucas, R.E. (1982): "Interest Rates and Currency Prices in a Two-County World", in: Journal of Monetary Economics, Vol. 10, p. 335-359.

Lütkepohl, H./Reimers, H.-E. (1992): "Impulse Response Analysis of Cointegrated Systems", in: Journal of Economic Dynamics and Control, Vol. 16, p. 53-78.

MacDonald, R./Taylor, M.P. (1992): "Exchange Rate Economics: A Survey", in: Staff Papers, International Monetary Fund, Vol. 39, p. 1-57.

MacKinnon, J.G. (1991): Critical Values for Cointegration Tests", in: Engle, R.F./Granger, C.W.J. (eds.): "Long-Run Economic Relationships: Readings in Cointegration". Oxford, p. 267-276.

Marston, R.C. (1988): "Exchange Rate Policy Reconsidered", in: Feldstein, M. (ed.): "International Economic Cooperation". Chicago, p. 79-136.

McElroy, M.B. (1977): "Goodness of Fit for Seemingly Unrelated Regressions: Glahn's R_{yx}^2 and Hooper's $\bar{r}^2$", in: Journal of Econometrics, Vol. 6, p. 381-387.

McKibbin, W./Sachs, J. (1988): "Comparing the Global Performance of Alternative Exchange Rate Arrangements", in: Journal of International Money and Finance, Vol. 7, p. 387-410.

McKinnon, R. (1988): "Monetary and Exchange Rate Policies for International Financial Stability: A Proposal", in: Journal of Economic Perspectives, Vol. 2, No. 1, p. 83-120.

Meese, R./Rogoff, K. (1983a): "Empirical Exchange Rate Models of the Seventies. Do They Fit Out of Sample?", in: Journal of International Economics, Vol. 14, p. 3–24.

Meese, R./Rogoff, K. (1983b): "The Out-of-Sample Failure of Empirical Exchange Rate Models: Sampling Error or Misspecification?", in: Frenkel, J.A. (eds.): "Exchange Rates and International Macroeconomics". Chicago, p. 67–105.

Meese, R.A. (1986): "Testing for Bubbles in Exchange Markets: A Case of Sparkling Rates?", in: Journal of Political Economy, Vol. 94, No. 21, p. 345–373.

Meese, R./Rogoff, K. (1988): "Was It Real? The Exchange Rate-Interest Differential Relation Over the Modern Floating-Rate Period" in: Journal of Finance, Vol. 43, No. 4, p. 933–948.

Miller, M./Williamson, J. (1987): "Targets and Indicators: A Blueprint for the International Coordination of Economic Policy". Washington, D.C.

Mussa, M. (1979): "Empirical Regularities in the Behavior of Exchange Rates and Theories of the Foreign Exchange Market", in: Carnegie-Rochester Conference Series on Public Policy, Vol. 11, p. 9–58.

Ng, S./Perron, P. (1993): "Unit Root Tests in ARMA Models with Data Dependent Methods for the Selection of the Truncation Lag". Mimeo, Department de Sciences Economique et C.R.D.E., Universite de Montreal, Quebec, Canada.

Obstfeld, M. (1984): "Balance-of-Payments Crises and Devaluation", in: Journal of Money, Credit, and Banking, Vol. 16, p. 208–217.

Obstfeld; M. (1985): "Floating Exchange Rates: Experience and Prospects", in: Brookings Papers of Economic Activity, Vol. 2, p. 369–450.

Obstfeld, M. (1986): "Rational and Self-fulfilling Balance-of-Payments Crises", in: American Economic Review, Vol. 76, No. 1, p. 72–84.

Ogaki, M./Park, J.Y. (1990): "A Cointegration Approach to Estimating Preference Parameters". Mimeo, University of Rochester, Rochester, New York, USA.

Osterwald-Lenum, M. (1992): "A Note with Quantiles of the Asymptotic Distribution of the Maximum Likelihood Cointegration Rank Test Statistics", in: Oxford Bulletin of Economics and Statistics, Vol. 54, No. 3, p. 461–471.

Pagan, A. (1984): "Econometric Issues in the Analysis of Regressions with Generated Regressors", in: International Economic Review, Vol. 25, p. 221–247.

Pantula, S.G. (1989): "Testing for Unit Roots in Time Series Data", in: Econometric Theory, Vol. 5, p. 256–271.

Perron, P. (1988): "Trends and Random Walks in Macroeconomic Time Series. Further Evidence from a New Approach", in: Journal of Economic Dynamics and Control, Vol. 12, p. 297–332.

Stock, J.H. (1992): "Unit Roots and Trend Breaks". Mimeo, Kennedy School of Government, Harvard University, Cambridge, Massachusetts, USA.

Stockman, A. (1987): "The Equilibrium Approach to Exchange Rates", in: Economic Review, Federal Reserve Bank of Richmond, March/April, p. 12–30.

Stockman, A. (1990): "Exchange Rates, the Current Account, and Monetary Policy", in: Haraf, W.S./Willet, T.D. (eds.): "Monetary Policy for a Volatile Global Economy". American Enterprise Institute. Washington, D.C., p. 95–116.

Tobin, J. (1978): "A Proposal for International Monetary Reform", in: Eastern Economic Journal, Vol. 4, p. 153–159.

Toda, H.Y. (1993): "Finite Sample Performance of Likelihood Ratio Tests for Cointegrating Ranks in Vector Autoregressions". Mimeo, Institute of Socio-Economic Planning, University of Tsukuba, Tsukuba, Japan.

Toda, H.Y. (1994): "Finite Sample Properties of Likelihood Ratio Tests for Cointegrating Ranks when Linear Trends are Present", in: Review of Economics and Statistics, Vol. 76, No. 1, p. 66–79.

West, K.D. (1987): "A Standard Monetary Model and the Variability of the Deutsch-Dollar Exchange Rate", in: Journal of International Economics, Vol. 23, p. 53–76.

Williamson, J. (1985): "The Exchange Rate System". Washington, D.C.

GPSR Compliance

The European Union's (EU) General Product Safety Regulation (GPSR) is a set of rules that requires consumer products to be safe and our obligations to ensure this.

If you have any concerns about our products, you can contact us on ProductSafety@springernature.com

In case Publisher is established outside the EU, the EU authorized representative is:

Springer Nature Customer Service Center GmbH
Europaplatz 3
69115 Heidelberg, Germany

Batch number: 10725973

Printed by Printforce, the Netherlands